MONTANA
Winter Days

Marjorie M. Snipes

Illustrations by Wayland Moore

Vabella Publishing
P.O. Box 1052
Carrollton, Georgia 30112
www.vabella.com

©Copyright 2014 by Marjorie M. Snipes

All rights reserved. No part of the book may be reproduced or utilized in any form or by any means without permission in writing from the author. All requests should be addressed to the publisher.

Cover art by Wayland Moore.

Back cover author photo by Frankie M. Snipes

Manufactured in the United States of America

13-digit ISBN 978-1-938230-75-2

Library of Congress Control Number 2014946255

10 9 8 7 6 5 4 3 2 1

To Mumsie and Joseph

Contents

List of Illustrations	vii
Preface	ix
The Calendar of Days	3
January (January 17 - January 31)	3
February (February 1 - February 28)	29
March (March 1 – March 31)	103
Acknowledgements	179

List of Illustrations

Frozen Pond	4
White-Tailed Deer and Dragons	7
Cowboy Pastor	10
School Bus Stop	13
Skiing	19
Snowflakes	22
Snow-Laden Trees	26
The Big Little Player	30
Ice Skating	36
The Cabin on the Hill	42
Making a Joyful Noise	46
A Very Montana Establishment	51
Cowboy Chocolates	56
Rodeo in Kalispell	61
The Winter Birthday Camp	66
Women at the Post Office	74
The Vet and Her Best Friends	78
The Logging Road	82
Man in a Jar	85
The Piano Lesson	91
The School Chef's Healthy Meals	98
Melting Snow	104
The Kilroy Wind	107
The Ebullient Piano Tuner	111
The (Former) Health Clinic	119
The Writing Place	123
Dirt Bike Dreams	125
The Garbage Dump	131
Highway Elk	136
Restaurant Trophies	141
A Wild Walk through the Wooly Woods	145

On Your Mark	148
Burgers and Basketball in a Bar	162
The Wallow	170
Spring Grass	174
Southbound	178

Preface

Travel changes our perspectives. I suspect this is why it has frequently been a component of adolescent rituals across diverse cultures. From the aboriginal "walkabout" to the excessive European "Grand Tour," sending young people abroad has often been seen as something edifying, purifying, and transformative. Yet the usefulness of travel, and by that I mean travel of substance – meaning, enough time to require you to get about the business of living in a different way, is even more beneficial as we age and consider our lives in their broadest arrays. Too often we accept the challenges of life as insurmountable hurdles and we stay in place, rooted. Yet change of place re-awakens the senses and the soul and opens new possibilities of living.

I am an anthropologist, and I have traveled widely over space and time, living years at a time in Peru and Argentina, studying things like religion, goat and sheep herding, and migration. I guess in a sense I got "broken in" right away, as I started traveling quite early in my life. But as I have aged and my family has grown now to include my son, a dog, and two cats, I have too quickly accepted that my traveling days are over. We take occasional weekend visits to interesting places and sometimes pack everyone into the car to go to Mumsie's house for holiday, but, overall, it has seemed too complicated to really travel again. Schedules are complicated, finding rentals where multiple species are acceptable is complicated, and getting breathing space from any profession is exceedingly complicated. But this year I decided that we had to at least attempt to overcome that physical inertia of moving only in place with no advance, like gerbils on a wheel. I was allotted a long-sought and long-awaited sabbatical during which I had several articles to complete, each of them requiring additional research, and I started making plans early. But while everything hinged on several axial points, an affordable rental in a place where I wanted to be was the most vexing. From May to October 2012, I searched fruitlessly. Mostly, people would simply not respond to my request for a rental for two adults, one child, two cats, and two dogs (including my mother's dog now). Then, in early November 2012, not more than eight weeks before the sabbatical would begin and thinking that this may not happen, I found a semi-rustic cabin, willing landlords, and an extraordinary town. We had been there before and knew some people, but we had not stayed there. Before, we had simply traveled through on weekends from time to time, heading to Missoula from a town further up the Valley. But I knew that this place was good enough for joy.

After securing the cabin, I began crafting a leave of absence for my son from his 5th grade class in Georgia. His teachers and principal quite literally rose to the occasion, intuitively aware that this opportunity was something valuable for everyone on both sides. Together, we arranged for him to be away for his third quarter, which meant he could leave and return as seamlessly as possible. We also arranged that he would be somewhat of a roving reporter, sending back comments and correspondences to his school, bridging places with words and stories. My mother traveled from her home in Virginia to Georgia to join up, and we left Carrollton, Georgia on January 12th, 2013 en route to Big Sky Country.

In anthropology we call the shift of perspective the "Rashomon Effect," based on the well-known Japanese movie *Rashomon* of Akira Kurosawa which tells about something violent that happened in a forest. Everyone who experienced this thing told a different version of what happened when they were later questioned, kind of like an Asian version of the "People's Court." As the film concludes, we are left very muddled and confused about reality and truth. At first we think we can discern between the different people's stories, but, at last, we acknowledge that each one of the stories is believable and possible. In fact, essentially each story as it is told did occur from the perspective of the protagonist who tells it. It leaves the viewer unsettled.

So what does all this have to do with travel and Montana? Well, for me, the greatest value of travel is that it forces me to shift the way I see things. Sometimes that shift is exhilarating and sometimes it is devastating, but when away from my life's usual ballasts, I turn more towards those internal ones and I learn that they guide me more surely. Living in Montana for some three months forced me to become watchful, insightful, and both more outward- and inward-oriented. I found people around me interesting and places around me deeply compelling. It forced me to constantly shift perspective, but instead of finding confusion and befuddlement, I began to sense something deeply truthful about life and people and place, something that was less centered on me and on what I knew to be true and more on what is, how we are all so much alike, and that we matter greatly to each other. There I met characters, played in strange and lovely scenes, and felt alive and deeply joyful in the way that we all feel when our senses are fully awakened. Sights, smells, sounds, tastes, and even textures changed in my world as I knew it.

For many people, three months might sound like a wee bit of time. For a college student or professor, it is not even a full semester. But it is an allotment of time that requires adaptation, and when we adapt, we re-position ourselves. I have had long days of travel overseas, but what I found on this trip reminded me that travel is mostly in the heart and mind. It is a process of re-opening those vessels to let in something unanticipated and unplanned. In *Out of Africa* when Denys

Finch-Hatton asks Karen Blixen/Isak Dinesen, one of the greatest storytellers of all time, if she has traveled to all these places that she talks about in her stories, she replies, "No, but I have been a mental traveler." Indeed, travel does not always mean physical movement, but true travel does always mean change. As people face hardships, daily challenges, and even joys in their lives, they travel. Travel is a condition of changing places, whether it is psychological, emotional, spiritual, or physical, and it signals that a shift is occurring. Sometimes sought after and sometimes thrust upon us, travel has deep and prolonged value for the human soul.

  The more and the better we travel, the greater we go beyond perspective and into that place in our hearts and minds where truth abides and we know something about who we are as a person and as a species. We become a people more compassionate and empathetic towards the condition of our collective lives, poised with untapped potential. Through travel, I more poignantly sense that the loss of my neighbor is in essence the loss of some aspect of my own self as well. This binds us and weaves us together into something common, knowable, and valued. As Washington Irving said, "There is a certain relief in change, even though it be from bad to worse; as I have found in traveling in a stage-coach, that it is often a comfort to shift one's position and be bruised in a new place." In experiencing the commonalities of what it means to be human, we make contact with the seeds of the future. Good or bad, they bring us closer to knowing what is true about ourselves and others.

  These reflections are simple and guttural by design, as I mostly wrote them in the mornings between 4:00-6:00 a.m. when the cabin was quiet (after I fed the cats, that is), when my worries were not yet awake, and my day's academic workload not yet on schedule. My chair faced East and looked out onto a large frozen lake. I always kept the blinds up on the windows so that I could see the first light and there were mornings when I experienced breath-taking sunrises. Some days I would go out for a walk and find that I had something to say afterward. I took each of these prompts seriously and shared my ponderings aloud on paper, although I sometimes changed a reflection when another more interesting one asserted itself later in the day. Some reflections are like a daily journal, but others are full-blown stories, those more often written later in the afternoons. All I can say is that they mostly came out that way. I wrote this primarily as a way of remembering the place and the people whom I have come to love so much in such a short time.

In Quechua, the *lingua franca* of the central Andes of Peru and Bolivia, there is a little word of which I was constantly reminded during my time in Montana. It filters through each of these pages. The word is *yapa*. It is primarily used in the Andes during market transactions when the customer asks the vendor to sell some amount of produce to an exceeding amount of the request, brimming full and overflowing. In Psalm 23:5, there is the familiar refrain, "My cup runneth over." When someone receives *yapa*, in essence they get just a little more than they asked for or deserved. Throughout our stay in this little valley in Montana, we received *yapa* on a daily basis.

Carrollton, Georgia

JANUARY

The Calendar of Days

Thursday, January 17: (20°F, low, cloudy; 40°F, high)

Winter is still time. Life is frozen, slowed down, waiting. Our pond is frozen. It does not shimmer, it does not reflect, it does not ripple. It sits in stagnant cold, caught in the act of movement, stilled. The trees stand as stately as ever, but they are now very patient sentinels, waiting, watching. Covered in "sprayed-on" globs of snow and gripping ice, they shimmer in the sun like a mirage, while remaining immobile and stark. The world is caught like a fish on the hook of winter. Only the sun defies time. It shines forth brilliantly and luxuriantly, throwing away warmth like potlatch coppers. It is frivolous and wasteful and arrogant. It breaks through the stillness and dares to move across the winter sky, threatening to melt away time, reminding us that it will win - eventually. Indoors, the cabin is cozy and creaks and moans in the burden of sheltering and providing. Inside, life prevails unafraid of the seriousness of time. It is almost a mockery of winter. But not quite, because around the door are the accoutrements…gloves, hats, scarves, wet socks and dripping boots, bulky coats that look like snowmen huddled expectantly to return outdoors. Winter is pressing all around.

Unlike the creatures of this place, I am an interloper who has come to engage with this harshness. I am not a Montanan by nature and I do not have past experiences to guide me through winter with sensibility and efficiency. I am not captive here by nature. Why, then, did winter draw me? Why did I seek self-imprisonment? Why does my heart quicken to breathe in this woody cold and this entrapment? Facing the frozen pond and merengue-covered lodgepole pines and the blinding sun, I cannot help but smile. Inside, I know this answer. I can feel it.

Frozen Pond

Friday, January 18: (14°F, low, cloudy; 40°F, high)

I have pondered this question about harshness: I come towards the harsh winter because there is something inside of me that recognizes it, something that knows life itself as a luxurious and fragile good - something fleeting and persistent to survive the onslaught of environment every day. But this winter state also reminds me of time and cyclical movements and the promise of renewal...soon, but *in its own time*. It is not helplessness but patience that sets the tone – waiting, expectant, trusting that something moves time outside of ourselves and we follow along. Whether we call it God or Natural Selection or Mother Nature, it decides and we conform. Perhaps it is the sense of joyful subordination and unburdening of responsibility? How can I plan and control my day if I am living at the behest of something else or some other sense of time? I become more watchful, more careful, more observant and more delicate. It is a very bearable lightness of being. It quiets the mind and body and awakens the soul and spirit to a state of responsive dependency. I am not used to this, but I recognize it.

This morning the cold is less biting at 14 degrees and the snow is now two days old. There is disregard in such snow, as it looks beguilingly white from afar, even while it is soiled by daily life: it accumulates deer droppings and urine stains, water drippings from trees that form into hard, translucent ground debris, little bits of green needles ripped apart by black squirrels frenzied to horde on sunny days. The dirty snow and warm days make me wish for more cold and a fresh coating of paint on the ground to make it look less dirtied than it really is - all the way down.

The clouds this morning are spurious – they are wisp-like, in slow motion, a reminder that the day is never as dormant as it seems. And the sun as it rises, casts color everywhere. This great ball of fire turns the world rosy, seducing us into seeing harshness as beauty, compelling us to look and sense awe. And yet it will soon withdraw the color and begin to cast shadows of darkness as well. I have been out in the world already to walk my dog and wait for the school bus to take my son away. The day is colder than it seems, but it allows us to be with it still. I embrace it and then turn back towards the cabin. I peek at it from inside, but I also re-set myself to go out again. Beauty is not only visual and presence is not only physical. It is also a relationship between things and the way they are connected. It is also dirty snow and cold winds.

Saturday, January 19: (11°F, low, sunny; 44°F, high)

I feel as if I have been cast back into an older world – one that has dense and layered connections with primordial nature. Yesterday seven deer came into the back area of the house and walked around impetuously, stopping periodically to turn their heads and glare at me, asking, "How dare you come into our territory, an uninvited and illegitimate guest?" Momentarily I felt unmasked, belittled, the true interloper that I am. I photographed them while they circled me and stared me down. I remained caught in the act as I temporarily shared their space without permission. At least they did not ask for identification – not yet anyway.

Then late in the afternoon as darkness fell, we became part of an ancient rite. A congregation began forming in the little town area – cars and people all drawn towards the center of the icy town as the sun retreated. We joined the vehicular procession and, like so many others, parked by backing into space that lined the small road downtown, narrowing that area into a small slushy track with eerie headlights all pointed into the space. In front of us and to the right, in the small parking lot of a little store, a hair salon, and a laundromat, there was a heaping mound of old Christmas trees almost 20 feet high surrounded by icy sculptures of dinosaurs, horses, dragons, and other creatures. And as the sun and cold descended, along the two-block route marched young schoolchildren carrying very colorful paper dragon heads with multicolored garland strips and adults peppered haphazardly among them holding aloft rag torches soaked in gasoline and flaming brilliantly against the forbidding dark and cold. As they passed, people pushed in closer to the streets and then followed behind the supplicants to the parking lot, where the torches were used to light the bonfire. At first it was silent, somber, sacred, but as the loud and intense flames leapt high into the black sky, spitting out orange sparks of resin and ash and roaring as they conjured forth light and heat, the small crowd of adults likewise shifted from solemnity to an outburst of cheerful conversation, while they huddled near the fiery mound. Children began racing each other and throwing snowballs, leaving their colorful dragon garlands crushed and bleeding amid the slush and milling feet. I was witness to an ancient pagan rite of transformation and found myself lightened in the midst of fire and laughter. They call it Winterfest, a celebration of all things cold and icy and threatening. Against this somber backdrop, there is joy and radiance.

White-Tailed Deer and Dragons

Sunday, January 20: (14°F, low, sunny; 38°F, high)

We live in a part of town called Dogtown. The sign on the road boldly announces this and then underneath, "Population: Increasing." The waitress at Pop's said she thought it was named this because "there used to be a lot of dogs down there," but I wonder about the metaphorical propensity of this word because what there is a lot of today are single-wide trailers, outbuildings, random fences, trucks and truck parts, and unidentified lumps everywhere, jewels hidden beneath the winter frosting. However, it is a very quiet place – there is little outside activity this time of the year and our cabin, made of huge, thick pines, sits like an anomaly in the very real neighborhood wilderness, neighbors on both sides - one with a Confederate flag in the window facing us. Everyone is nice when we see them, even the *Confederados*. On the other side of the street is a small frozen lake for sale, surrounded on all sides by lodgepole pines. But from the front windows, we are apparently alone in our wilderness valley. The only view we see ahead is the frozen lake.

Today we went to church and reunited with people we knew when we were last here seven years ago. We did not live in this area then, but we did come into this town every Sunday for church, the weekly mail, and perishable supplies. Friendly, caring, self-subsistent, and outgoing, everyone greeted us genuinely and made us again one of them. It is a true privilege to be taken in as a wayfarer by full-timers. Most church members are loggers of some sort, but they also serve as the town's volunteer firemen, EMTs, and social workers. Serving others is their definition of Christian love. So as we come through and sit quietly on a bench in their church, they see us as no different than any other neighbor. Men dressed in pressed and creased blue jeans, Western shirts, and shined leather cowboy boots and women in assorted pressed pants and snow boots, their welcoming smiles and communion are as real as the stunning mountain views all around us. Pastor had on a brown-checked Western shirt with snaps and ribbing, coordinated brown jeans and cowboy boots. His message was about life ministry and he defined it as service outside of the church. It was practical and fundamental to faith. And in looking on such unpretentious humility, he served aptly as the role model of his own sermon. In his final prayer, he confessed that he knew his sermon was not as good as it should have been and he prayed that God would give him better words to serve, and tears began wetting my cheeks. When we live in deep community, rising above and competing does not render success. Quiet service and humility do.

Marjorie M. Snipes

Cowboy Pastor

Monday, January 21: (20°F, low, partly cloudy; 35°F, high)

Last night we went to the high school to hear a so-called West African drumming group from Missoula traveling through the rural valleys of Montana. They were performing and then working the following days with young people in the schools in percussion workshops. The lead percussionist was from a small town in the Flathead Valley area, across our Mission Mountain range, and he thanked everyone for coming to hear them. But as he talked about this town, he told them that he loved this whole area of Montana. He said he loved taking his sons out fishing on Flathead Lake and seeing the rugged wilderness and then, "Wow! How lucky we are to live in this cool place!" Everyone clapped. And I was struck by this different type of bonding with place. I don't doubt that "home" is beautiful to all people everywhere and I don't doubt that beautiful places are created in the mind's eye, even in the darkness of urban alleyways, but how different it was to me to witness a town priding itself not on what it has done to "self-improve," but on what Mother Earth has provided. What an oddity to witness people universally in agreement that they were luckier than anyone else in the country because they lived here. Even unemployed loggers struggling to feed their families clapped and smiled. At least they had this. And this was quite a lot to have from their point of view. It was more than enough, I agree.

When the group called for the intermission, some 75 people filed into the school's lobby to view an exhibition of photographs that an artist had made of their town, their houses, and their mountains. Here place asserts itself as a primary agent. One person even found her home in a photograph. Is beauty when we see ourselves through others' eyes or is it truly in the eye of the beholder? This is a hard thing to answer and conjures up many other thoughts. I wonder about those who first saw this

Valley and first lived here. Did they see what I see? Did it move them as much as it does me?

Tuesday, January 22: (4°F, low, sunny; 26°F, high)

Cold can be as enticing as warmth. From our cabin hilltop, the big sky view is tremendous. This morning the sun comes forth, hazed over by clouds and frigidness below, yet it proclaims itself boldly, convinced of its mission to take on today. Over the solid-surfaced lake in our front window, there are small, low-lying clouds of white. Is the surface warmer than the air or vice versa? They meet somewhere in the middle, very visible and not yet worked out.

My son and I waited for ten minutes this morning at the end of the drive, looking for the lighted yellow school bus rumbling over the icy road. The dog stood beside me on her leash. Stillness, biting cold around us, but we shared our hopes for the day with each other. Our small, tinny voices felt like little prayers. Beginnings are always hopeful, always a little thrilling. At last we saw the bus and waved goodbye, as each took the next step for today. We will meet again once the sun passes its mid-mark.

I walked with the dog up the long, icy driveway, the cabin lights seeming to wink at me that they had a warm commodity waiting. My mother and I would now be able to share a cup of coffee without watching the clock. Outward and inward times are not always the same. Each moves at its own pace. The school bus demands that we be waiting at the end of our drive between 7:20 and 7:30 every morning, but after we meet that demand, there is an allotted space before another demand asserts itself. That space opens to inward time. I often wonder which is better. Is it better to be attuned inward to outward time (or outward to inward time)? Or is the best life one in which we can alternate time zones at will to remind ourselves that time controls only a bit but need not take over? The cats meet me at the door. Ah, they are a tribute to alternative time. I smile. Another little whispered answer.

School Bus Stop

Wednesday, January 23: (13°F, low, partly cloudy; 29°F, high)

The word *community* is charged in ways many of us have forgotten, I imagine. At least I have. *Commune* is to share or move between people. It is connection, a force that binds and clusters and weaves together.

Here *community* takes on its root word meaning in a way that it does not in many larger places. The school is called a *community* school, which means that adults filter in and out of the doors all day using equipment and space for community events. After the school shooting at Sandy Hook in Newtown, CT, we have heard so much about fortifying the schools and arming teachers to defend themselves and their students against outsiders, yet here in this little town, there are no outsiders. The school defines itself not as a fortress but as a learning membrane of sorts. The front door is unlocked and the ante room is there only because it buffers cold air and wet shoes from the warm hallways. That door is also unlocked. And the main office, which is at the front, is turned so that virtually nothing in the front door area disturbs the work there. Indiscriminate adults walk in and out throughout the day, one of them me.

My son needed a place to practice piano. The school welcomed us to come and practice there, so I now meet him after school right outside his classroom and then we walk together to the "multi-purpose room," where the ancient black upright Steinway & Sons sits in a corner, somewhat forgotten, except as a flat surface for piling props for the latest theatrical offering, scratched and squeaky. We pull it out, re-purpose it for music, and sit there somewhat undisturbed for an hour a day. I say somewhat because every day at least one adult comes in and gets things to use in the adjoining room – one day it was bells for the community chorus to play, another day it was cross-country ski equipment for families in the community, and another day it was props for the school theater group. Right now they are in the process of building a climbing wall there in front of the cafeteria tables. Funny how strangely wonderful it is to say that the school *comes alive* after the students leave. Basketball games erupt in the gym, groups start practicing for some future event, and people filter in and out talking and enjoying themselves.

It is the same with the high school. The public library and the high school library are the same, and many days I go and write there during school hours. High school students come in and out for projects and sit beside the community public on internet and at work tables, everyone engaged in their work. I hear snippets and whole conversations about someone looking for work, the record of the high school basketball team, a woman trying to rebuild her cabin after a tree fell on it, a young man's essay for a university scholarship, the week's articles in the local newspaper, history assignments that take a long time to complete, and the weather. Occasionally a student finds her parent in the library and they have a personal conversation before the student returns to class. It is very collegial and very colloquial. Life is more seamless and less fractured than I have experienced before. It is whole and connected. I wonder what it is like to think in the 9th grade that you will be in this library for the rest of your life. Does it make a person more mindful of resources and more appreciative? Does it make a student more civic-minded? Does it make all of us more aware of each other and less divided? Does it help blend our lives so that we are community and not communi*ties*?

Thursday, January 24: (32°F, low, freezing rain; 40°F, high)

In the library I sit and face a small window and beside it is a large map of former Indian territories of Montana plastered on it in red. Outside of former Indian lands, Montana hardly exists at all. And yet when they mark the current reservation boundaries, the state looms large and menacingly. Boundaries, frontiers, lines – they serve to structure things and give them a physical presence. But what they de-*sign*-ate is ultimately small, because the essence of what they seek to contain is uncontainable. Take the former Indian lands – they are erased and re-marked, but their legacy does not retract into the smaller space. Who and what we were is always part of who and what we are. This is how identity is constructed – bits and pieces amidst the debris of our past and the formalities of our present. When viewed as marks on paper, boundaries look like colorful amusements and noisy pronouncements, but they are not trivial and they always cost much; they are human playthings and they impose and endure only as long as the force to defend them does. They are pencil marks on earth's continuity. It is kind of like in the South in early spring when small clusters of daffodils appear out of nowhere shouting in yellow that someone used to live in this now-vacant place. Nothing sits around the flowers and there is no trace of the house that once stood there. Nothing else is left – just a temporarily modified nature. Interesting that something so intrusive can leave behind something so beautiful. I guess it goes both ways, though. Maps are kind of like daffodils to me. They loudly proclaim something that happened a long time ago, usually. And those lines, sometimes colorful and pretty to look at, just as often symbolize someone's lost home and lost place in the world. Isn't this odd?

Friday, January 25: (28°F, low, morning snow; 39°F, high)

Snow delights us. I know everyone does not respond uniformly to it, but faces of both children and adults display unexpected delight in the earliest winter snows. When we arrived at the elementary school to meet my son's teacher last week, it was a Thursday, and Thursdays are special in Montana. Schoolchildren get out early on Thursdays so that they can do some kind of unique sport activity, and this quarter it is Nordic skiing. We arrived to the school right after the morning bell and planned on him starting the following day, Friday. But as we met person after person, all of whom called my son by name eagerly waiting his forecast arrival to their school, everyone enthusiastically told us that he should start "right now, at this minute" because that afternoon the children had Nordic skiing on the public trails. So last week was my son's first-time-ever on skis. Heck, it was really the first time he saw genuine snow!

Yesterday my son went skiing for the *second* time, now convinced he was a pro. In fact, he was thrilled that they let him move from the Beginners to the Intermediates yesterday (the Beginners in Montana are usually only first- and second-graders). The teachers and parents load them all up on the school bus with donated skis and poles and boots and they get off at the trailheads and divide up by level of difficulty, all grouped under an adult. Each child must know how to put on boots and clip on skis for him or herself. That is the deal. And the trails – there are several of them – are well-groomed and take the kids through a magical forest of ponderosas, lodgepoles, birches, and true bounty of nature. How could they not grow up environmentalists and conservators when they see what they have to lose? I photographed while the 40 or so children, 2nd grade to 8th, cajoled me to "grab a pair of skis" and join them! Something in me ached to join up.

The school loans out all their donated equipment on Friday afternoons to parents and community members who want to use it, as long as they return it Monday morning. A year before, two of the parents wrote a grant to the sports store REI to ask for ski equipment for *their* school. When REI chose the grant and offered to donate everything they needed, these forward-thinking and community-minded parents asked that the donation be made in monies so that the school could purchase the same equipment through two very small local sports businesses in the town that were hurting economically. REI agreed and so the grant benefitted the school and community equally. Wow. Isn't that remarkable? Here the school is a community resource in the fullest sense of the word. One of the teachers told me that they wanted everything in use as much as possible. "It is meant to be used, not stored. It belongs to us all!"

Skis, poles, bipeds sliding across a wonderland, a magical forest, and everyone urging each other to "join up" – this is a place where spirit, soul, and imagination run deep, where people trust and bond with each other, where each species sticks together not just for survival, but for delight as well. How beautiful to find joy in and through one another.

Skiing

Saturday, January 26: (33°F, low, rain, patchy fog, then sun; 39°F, high)

On Saturdays we travel out of our small town for two things: groceries and piano lessons. Destination: Missoula, Montana.

Missoula is a provisioner's paradise. It is like converging onto a giant spaceship from all the outer reaches! All the many small towns around the valleys pour out and into Missoula for provisions on Saturdays. As we make our way south and then westward, we are in a large stream of cars and trucks heading to the depot area. And in Missoula there appear to be millions of people and cars and a great shortage of parking places everywhere! Car washes are running steadily, gas lines form, and the Wal-Mart parking lot contains large numbers of "fishermen" looking for parking places for their rigs. It is a vehicular rodeo.

As we drove around part of the fray ourselves, little bits of ice and rock and salt pelted at the car. Everyone had intermittent wipers going, and occasionally you'd see the washer fluid spew out and clear off a section of windshield, even as they stayed dirty and splotched and quickly blinded back over again. Muddy, wet roads just like any cattle town in the West. Chaotic convergence of need and mass cultural confusion as newbies sought to negotiate endlessly marked one-way streets.

There is a lightness in the air of Missoula, everyone there for a specific purpose and all getting about their business as well as they can in such crowds. People everywhere. People busy. People getting stocked up for another week or another month or another year. I feel like part of a wagon train pulling into Dodge City to get provisions for the next part of the drive. After the quiet contemplation of many days in the small Valley town, Missoula was rowdy, unkempt, and had the feel of a lawless Wild West town, where the sheriff's main job was just to keep us moving on through as soon as possible in hopes that we'd take Chaos along with us as we left.

Sunday, January 27: (27°F, low, light snow; 34°F, high)

This morning we woke to a frilly light snow like fine pieces of Belgian lace floating through the air. The ground had about an inch of new-fallen snow, and the falling flakes glinted and winked playfully in the early morning sun. Magic and quiet have descended again. I am palpably reminded that we are back in the magical forestland on the Valley floor, long away from the city of yesterday.

I sat on the porch this morning in the cold and was soothed by the utter silence all around. Even with neighbors and a road nearby, no one was stirring this Sunday morning. All quiet on the Western front, both the Mission and Swan mountain ranges equally hidden by low-lying snow clouds. This morning, in fact, we do not have neighbors at all – our view is enveloped in the snow clouds and fog. We live inside this little place suddenly all by ourselves. How easily Mother Nature erases each of us! Here yesterday, gone today! But, alas, each of us encounters our world alone as well – our experience, our feelings, our consciousness. Sometimes we do not like being here all alone, but we are. Well…but…there is that massive Presence that also sits with us, beside us, inside us, and around us. Alone, but not quite – alone enough to make us know that we are responsible for our lives, but not enough to feel hopeless. We still reach out to each other. We still seek ourselves in the other. "Hey, don't you feel just like I do?"

Which always brings me back to silence. Silence is so precious to me – it is the point where I must look at me and say, "How do you feel? Why do you feel?" Here, now, I make friends with me. And, today for a few minutes, if I look around me, I am the only one in the world.

Marjorie M. Snipes

Snowflakes

Monday, January 28: (14°F, low, intermittent light snow; 34°F, high)

Our cats and dogs have doubled in size since getting here! Their weight has not changed, but their bodies are now covered with a heavy, luxurious fur that would cause envy among minks and martens everywhere. Each little creature has become an angora! The cats' white fur bristles out with multiple velvety layers and they stalk through the cabin as if a grizzly might be in the kitchen. The dogs, permanently tired, have also increased their wool weight, nappy pelage rippling along their backs and sides and a pronounced ruff forming around their necks. Our cabin is as warm as our house down South, but their bodies know we are not there. Their bodies anticipate the day that the heat runs low and we are forced to give up our artificial lives and become authentic animals again. Clearly, the cats and dogs will be ready. Me, not as much. I fear that of all the species inhabiting my house, I am the least prepared, the one who envisions far more control than I actually have, the one whose life is the most illusionary of them all.

Tuesday, January 29: (21°F, low, intermittent snow, Winter Storm Advisory; 28°F, high)

It started snowing again yesterday afternoon, light showers of fine lace. It was not terribly cold, but there was a clear sense that winter was asserting itself again after such nice, sunny days and lack of a firm commitment. But this snow is different. It is wetter and heavier and grabs hold of your shoes, mittens, and hats hitching a ride anywhere you go. And it does not drift – it blankets, covering up all the debris of well-lived days and taking over again as the primary natural force, erasing all human activity completely, as if we were never here. The trees, having shed their white skins, are now covered again and huddle underneath their cold blankets. The sky this morning is a stony grey and hangs low, the only evidence of the bright and cheery sun is a dusky grey light over a white world. We have about two fresh inches this morning, but Missoula radio says there is more on the way. Although the roads are always remarkably good for conditions, the radio reports that they are "predictably unpredictable" this morning. The announcers chat like the old friends they are, and the callers form part of that community. Here I think familiarity does not so much breed contempt as trust.

Yesterday as I waited for my son after school, the parents talked together and two were kidding each other about scrawling messages on dirty car sides and pulling jokes on each other. And I came in carrying the skis we had borrowed over the weekend and simply walked through the school, passing classrooms as I went to the multi-purpose room to self-check them back in (meaning, I crossed out my name on a clipboard).

No one noted who entered the school or what they were bringing. Teachers passed me in the hallway with the skis and smiled. This is a kind of life I may have never known before – even as a child. Does extending trust breed trust? It seems it does.

Wednesday, January 30: (21°F, low, snow all day, Winter Storm Advisory; 35°F, high)

    I went out this morning at 5:00 a.m. It was snowing lightly, as it has been for hours, and 21 degrees. We are still under the Winter Storm Advisory until this evening. But this snow does not seem so much threatening as it does peaceful. It is quiet and blanketing softly, even as the ground rises up with accumulation. My heart surges to meet this magical world this morning. Living in my artificial and self-contained inhabitation more regularly than I would like, the biting cold and slight sting of flakes on my face remind me that nature is vivacious and incessant.

    Snow is very interesting because it casts a kind of light from contrast. All the darkness outside, but there is a glow emanating from the snowed-over pond and within the thinner parts of the forest. This is a reflection from the waning gibbous moon and stars, hidden behind the clouds, but not so far that they do not continue to influence how we see. On the darkest nights, though, snow does go black. As light recedes, our world becomes a black, white, and grey palette, where our own eyes, too much accustomed to color, struggle to focus. I imagine the deer somewhere near, watching.

    Late last week a little boy from here only four years old was outside playing and fell into a half-frozen quarry pond. His tiny body was retrieved late into the night, while his family mourned grievously. The pastor of the church where we have been attending was the chaplain and EMT on call and he has been visibly shaken all week. We hear often of broken bones, snowmobile accidents, car fatalities and near-misses in this world of rough weather and predators like grizzly, black bear, and bobcat. Already we have witnessed two rescues in the wilderness around the town, one of a snowmobiler and his son lost overnight and the other of a college-age hiker who apparently lost his way as well. There is a sense of survival in living here at all. But coincident with this life that is so much more present in nature is the constant reminder that we must seek softness and forgiveness in ourselves and others and not in the wild. I am reminded that this is not just a place where weary Easterners come to reflect about life; this is also a place where beautiful daily life requires vigilance and wisdom. Little boys must learn these things to survive. Now grief blankets the town as well as snow. The school has put up a bulletin board with his pictures because he was a pre-K student there and the businesses have flyers everywhere for people to donate money to his family because the helicopter life-flight to Missoula, which did not save the little boy's life, cost more than $20,000. Is this the price of life? This loss reminds everyone that winter, snow, and ice are not playthings. It is not an inert scene of delight. Sadness suffuses the whiteness on these days.

Thursday, January 31: (32°F, low, snow continuing; 35°F, high)

It has snowed continually now for 48 hours and accumulated more than a foot. All of our play, walking, and tromping yesterday – even our small snowman – has been enveloped into bigger mal-shaped, nondescript fluffy mounds.

Where we once saw seedlings, rocks, and footsteps, we now see a sea of white with undulating waves marking mysterious objects. The "wet" snow has clung to the trees and turned them into a Christmas scene so absurdly snow-laden that it looks as if a child took a can of spray flakes and wastefully emptied a whole container on each tree. The trees stand mournful as their limbs have been lowered to their sides, no longer rising to meet the sky. From time to time, though, they spring to life as their burdens unexpectedly slide off, reminding us that even suffering has its limits. A quick movement occurs, it distracts us and we look, and we see a tree stretching itself somewhat back into shape for a few hours.

We partially cleared our driveway yesterday to liberate the car for no reason except habit, but today we are starting out even further behind. Alas, it may be useless to try this again. We are here and in place. So be it.

I wonder, though, about the deer. I have not seen them for two days. Are they someplace else waiting it out or are they inside one of those mysterious white mounds in the front yard?

Snow-Laden Trees

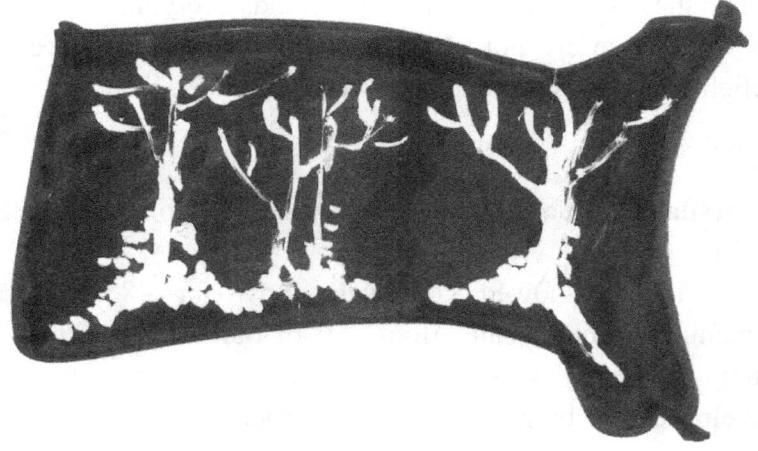

FEBRUARY

Montana Winter Days

Friday, February 1: (32°F, low, snow; 36°F, high)

Here Basketball is King. Even at the elementary school, the gym stays occupied almost continuously during daylight hours with winter girls' teams practicing, scrimmaging, and playing season games with small teams from as far as four hours away. The small elementary school actually has three teams: A team (7th and 8th graders), B team (6th and 7th graders), and C team (5th and 6th graders), each with only the minimum number of required players and no bench sitters available.

During games, the bleachers are pulled out in the gym and a small window is opened right at the entrance door. Tickets are free, but the concession stand sells nachos, hot dogs, fresh movie popcorn, sodas, and cookies for the many community members and parents who come to watch the girls play. And the games are tough. Small, slight little figures decked out in big shoes and polyester uniforms that engulf them run down the court opening space as they push forward toward the goal. One of the best players is a forward who is in the 5th grade. She is smaller than her teammates but makes up for her size by being very wily and quick. Opponents are hard-pressed to block her, as she moves the ball from hand to hand and backs up to get out of dead ends. Sometimes she shoots, but her important contribution is to grab the ball and move it quickly to her teammates who are taller and can shoot at much closer range because of her actions. She is a joy to watch and makes me think of a prairie dog that stands up, sees where the ball is, grabs it and moves it quickly through obstruction to get it to another location.

These games provide entertainment for everyone on snowy afternoons. The warm, boisterous environment, rich, buttery popcorn smells, and lively action draw in lots of viewers. If this is elementary school, I can only imagine what the high school games are like. And how well stocked those concession stands must be.

It has snowed now for some 60 hours, although there were periods of rain yesterday mixed in.

The Big Little Player

Saturday, February 2: (27°F, low, partly cloudy, clearing; 38°F, high)

When you are away, the sadness from home is much deeper and sharper. Instead of feeling alienated and cut off from it, you feel helpless and irresponsible, as if you had intentionally left this burden for someone else to carry, someone less fortunate and unable to be away from it. On mornings like these, the snow and the trees and the frozen lake all seem as foreign as if I were not here at all. I look at them as if they were a postcard of someone else's home. Not mine. Feelings and emotions are stilted and stiff and do not flow. My heart feels tight and heavy and beauty eludes me. I wonder if home primarily means "the place where burdens are meant to be carried." Heaviness does not feel the same way when we are not at home. It feels heavier and with fewer hand-holds.

I wandered yesterday looking for space. I wandered to the library and eventually to the church. But I never rested and my mind never focused on what it needed to consider. It felt weary all of a sudden. What do we learn of strangers and pilgrims as we travel on long journeys? I think we learn that home itself may be only an illusion because we assume control there that we really do not have anywhere. It is just that there we have habits so well ingrained that we can distract ourselves from our own thoughts. Here we cannot do that. Alive and alert, all of our senses enliven us and also torment us when they are uneasy. As a Christian I wonder if God wishes for me to know this torment as what is normal and necessary to having a conscious and committed life. I wonder.

Sunday, February 3: (14°F, low, partly cloudy; 36°F, high)

I heard this week that one of my former students, a young man who was very bright and hopeful about his future when I knew him, was tried on crimes he committed in July 2011. I had heard about the crime at that time and had let it only occasionally re-enter my mind. But this week he came up for trial for shooting three women. One was shot in the back and died instantly, one was shot in the front and paralyzed, and the other was shot in the front and survived physically intact. My student was working as a parking attendant, having just graduated and now facing what the next step would be. And in ten minutes of stupidity, he made his life's permanent decision. I heard from the news reporters that he had been angry and somewhat listless. Angry about what? Well, he was mad at his employer, frustrated at home, and then he said in the trial that he had learned hatred from his classes on slavery and felt a need to do something about it that day of the crime. What did he do? He did just what the slave traders and plantation owners did – he made a decision that all humans were not one species and that one group was less human and should be debased and defamed. He denied individuality and agency to each of his victims as he became a slave trader himself. He purchased each of these unwilling victims himself and tied them to his life in perpetuity. Pain ties people together much more tightly than joy, but the bad can become unbearably heavy.

I have been deeply disturbed about hearing this again this past week through e-mails from colleagues. I knew that young man and could not grasp him in my mind any longer. He loomed as a monstrous and inhumane thing. Then yesterday, while we were in Missoula, I was able to see part of the trial streamed on internet and hear what he had to say. And as desperate and despicable and sickening as it all was and is, I watched my young student speak and I felt solace. He was still the young man I thought I knew – he spoke in the same quiet and mannered demeanor and described what happened as a period of time when he felt he was in a trance. This soothed me in a surprising way, as I recognized that person speaking and knew him to be as human as I. In that moment, across all the madness, sacrilege, and desecration, I wanted to hug him. I wanted him to understand that the most radical act against hatred and slavery is love – I wanted to read to him from Martin Luther King Jr.'s *Strength to Love* and explain to him how love is the only revolution that sticks. I wanted him to open his mind and heart and heal himself of these things. I wanted to turn back the clock and stand between him and this act. I hurt for his victims and their families, for his family, and... for him.

I heard that the jury went out to deliberate for 30 minutes only. They returned with the verdict that he was guilty on all counts charged. He would be given life in prison. As his father pleaded for parole, I turned off the news account. What does it mean to be in prison for life? Are we not all inside prisons of some sort? Is not our difference that I have every day to try to release myself from my weaknesses? Is not our difference that I have the moral duty to open and lose any chains that are self-inflicted? Is he not also imprisoned by those bars as well? Is he then inside a double prison?

Monday, February 4: (34°F, low, very light snow; 41°F, high)

This is a little "treehouse" town. It is truly that they cannot see the forest for the trees! Every road in town is named after trees: Redwood, Spruce, Locust, Larch, Cottonwood, Tamarack, Elm, Pine, Juniper, Cedar, Sequoia. A seething diversity of species all woven together in a grid marking boundaries of identity and ownership. Each house is situated really right there among the tree lines. When I was a little girl I lived on a street called "Singing Pines Drive." I always thought this was funny and wondered when it was that the pines would sing. I would go outside in summer and winter and sit very still, listening. They never sang to me as a little girl. But long after we moved from there and even after I had my own house in Georgia, I began to hear them sing. Now, as the winds rise up from the Gulf and begin passing through, I thrill to hear the pines' song. It is sweet and grave, as if it alone knows the stories of long ago. They are the humpback whales of the forest – moaning and creaking to a rhythm no one else hears.

    Today I went to lunch at The Filling Station and stopped in a little store beside it to mill about a minute. And as soon as I walked in someone said, "Hello, Marjorie!" I looked, and in the seconds before I recognized who was greeting me, I heard, "It's Ann, from the ice skating pond." You see, I went out ice skating yesterday. The last time I went ice skating was 37 years ago when we lived in Banner Elk, NC, where it would get cold enough to freeze shallow water. Every winter I would layer-bathe our back concrete slab over and over until I developed at least an inch or more of ice. Then I would skate over and over and around and around, dizzying myself as I went in circles from tracing the small rectangular block no more than 8 x 14 feet. I got good at taking on corners quickly and always figured that I would be a good hockey player if I had to be. But no one played hockey in that area. No one else skated either – just me. My family would graciously consent to using the front and side doors during the winter while I maintained the rink.

    When I got here, I heard there was an outside pond run by the Lion's Club. They kept it cleared and also kept a small shed with donated skates which anyone could borrow. At first I didn't consider it, as I am twice the size I was at 15 and half as limber. But then last week we accidentally met with the pond on a drive-around after church and I got this craving that was delightful. Do I dare? I borrowed skates for my son and taught him while I stood in snow boots, because the Lion's had no skates to fit me in the shed, and then the next day I drove to Missoula to find a pair for me. The sports stores were just too expensive, so I went by a secondhand store and found one pair of skates for sale and they were in my size! "Clearly, this is a very important sign," I thought. And yesterday I took the skates out on the ice with me attached and we went skating! My toes were tensed and clinching and my arms stayed out to the sides to steady my nerves, and I did fall one time, but I skated! I circled at least five times around an area twenty times bigger than my old concrete slab. How glorious! Even falling made me laugh and made me more confident because I realized that falling would not hurt me any more than anything else.

    Ann was there with her grand-daughter. It was her third time skating. She was more graceful than I was, but I laughed all over the ice. How curious and amusing it must have been for her to see a large woman with big feet skating across the ice and doing a slow circle in the middle! I like to think Ann remembered me because I brought some amusement to the pond that day. I wonder what stories she will tell about me. I wonder if she is writing lines tonight as I write mine, pondering on why some people choose ridiculous activities and do them for joy and without shame.

Ice Skating

Tuesday, February 5: (28°F, low, heavy snow; 41°F, high)
    This is a place of great intimacy between all things. The people know each other and understand each other's natures, something I find very foreign in my own world. The people know and have intimacy with the land and animals, as most are

hunters, loggers, and sundry other types of outdoorspeople. But the landscape itself creates an intimacy as well. The Valley is rich and hilly and covered with trees and it seems to swallow up its inhabitants in a close and primeval way. But instead of feeling trapped and suffocated, the meadows seem to nurture and nestle life. Surrounding all this thick and luscious richness are stark and towering peaks – on one side the Swan Mountains always snow-capped and usually also wrapped in thin clouds of fog and on the other side the Mission Mountains very harsh and rugged. And in between these immensities, in the long, water-logged Valley, lakes run along and connect by creeks and rivers like a string of pearls from tip to toe.

Tonight we went on a "night walk," a sort of journey of discovery using our different senses. Our eyes stayed widely open, but we were mostly informed by the wind on our cheeks and the curious depressions as we felt our way through snow. As long as we remained on the packed back road, then we could make progress, but as soon as we inadvertently stepped out of the tracks, we knew – we sunk down at least 15 inches into snow and felt ice droplets trickle into our boots and tickle our legs.

We saw three deer silhouettes along the trail as we walked – they were dark blots against the sky and snow. We were no more than 20 feet away and they stood and stared as long as we did. They still consider us strangers in their world, but we find them less and less strange every day. I like these night walks and wonder why I do not engage a sense of discovery in my own backyard in Georgia. Night changes everything, and in a world in which night has the undeserved burden of carrying fear and loneliness, how beautiful to engage it with delight instead and to move into it just like one of the animals.

Wednesday, February 6: (28°F, low, sprightly snow, partly sunny; 41°F, high)

Human beings are really owners by nature. We inhabit, colonize, settle down, and stay, even though we may move a lot in the meantime. We do not seem to know what to do with passersby. We cannot invest in them, cannot count on them, cannot plan for a future with them – they are just temporary fillers in our lives and we do not place much meaning in things we cannot hold and own and box. They confuse us and disorient us and sometimes even annoy us. What can I do with someone who only fits for a little bit in my life?

Recently I have had two incidents of being reminded of my transitory status and its effect on others. I went to a beautiful book reading a few evenings ago at a local store, where the small devoted "arts group" all knew each other and had an easy-going, relaxed manner chatting beforehand. When I entered I garnered a great deal of looks, but very quickly I was greeted warmly, asked my name, and invited to the small refreshment table to meet people. Before I filled them in, they began to delightedly share how thrilled they were that I had joined them and how active they were as a group. They gave me a preview of the evening reading and quickly updated me on future readings, going out of their way to let me know that I was very welcome, they were pleased to have me, and they looked forward to seeing me at all the events. Then someone asked me where I was from, since in a town this size they already knew I was the outsider who had not been here before, but had been seen "around town" for a few weeks. I told them who I was, generally why I was in Montana, where I was from (all of which they nodded approval to) and then that I would be here about two more months and looked forward to these occasions. All of sudden their faces froze. The e-mail tablet onto which they were excitedly writing my contact information was held aloft and mid-air for several uncomfortable seconds and their demeanors changed to momentary confusion, as they each grappled to interpret the full meaning of my statement. I felt like a fraud, as if I had shared an embarrassing secret in public. Quickly, they re-engaged with me, but they no longer had as much interest. Little by little people began pulling away to start their own conversations with other more permanent wayfarers. I made my way to a seat for the talk and a lady in front turned and said she was from Great Falls and also didn't come to many of these. We were clearly frozen out not because of our looks or money but because we were not people who lived here.

    Then yesterday I met up with the father of some friends of my son. He had heard about me and was excited to meet me. We spoke animatedly about where I was from and where he was from, and then he began to share things about how much he loved this place. He especially loved to go camping in the National Forests, teaching his sons how to set up camp, hunt, fish, and enjoy being outside and rely on themselves. Then he told me that he liked my son and enjoyed seeing how well the boys played together and asked me if I would consider letting him take my son with his boys to go camping this summer. He began saying how much my son would enjoy it and how much he could teach him about the outdoors. And then I interjected that I would love that and surely my son as well, but that we would only be here about two more months. A shadow and confusion passed over his face and he quickly said, "Oh, I didn't know you were only here a little while." He seemed disappointed and disturbed, as if these budding friendships may not be worth the investment. I again felt as if I were perpetrating fraud on good, decent people.

I wonder why the inability to think ahead in the future about someone changes our relationship. I certainly understand the emotion and have suffered its effects frequently in romantic relationships with people I have met while traveling. We must struggle to convince ourselves that we will stay in contact and visit with some regularity and then the normal means of knitting together our lives goes forward. But if we cannot do this, then we begin backing off from each other awkwardly, as if inconstancy were a contagious and frightening disease.

I suspect that this awkwardness reveals something very deep and fundamental about humans. Not only do we see ourselves as owners, but we are also poorly prepared to be fully alive and present at any given time. We can feel as if we are fully present and fool ourselves only as long as someone temporary and appealing does not pass through. It is the outsider who reveals our deepest inside nature. It is the outsider who challenges us to acknowledge that ownership is transitory and impermanence is enduring.

Thursday, February 7: (21°F, low, mostly clear; 41°F, high)

The little cabin we are in is very snug and upright. It is filled with amenities and niceties and pleasantries, but living in other people's things is awkward and worrisome. Things are breakable and bendable and exhaustible. In our own homes, we know the list of those things that need special treatment, those things that have only measurable life left in them, and those things that are simply ornery and must be handled in a sequence of steps to make them work properly.

But in other people's spaces, we do not know this history. We treat things as knowable and duplicated and inanimate, but things are really not always transferable. They, like us, come with histories. And sometimes, the lighter we live in place the more we damage it. Small and soft movements with a microwave, for example, can break the door, as it is more accustomed to be shut quickly and properly so that it pushes up the latch inside. Flicking lights on harshly causes them to come on immediately, while slow, careful switching translates into a small delay in the current reaching the fixture. Sitting lightly on the bed tips it, but jumping in roughly and without regard makes it level out and sleep well.

Perhaps there is a lesson in this. Perhaps our lives are much like these things – living fully and in commitment to what is before us, without regard or reservation, without concern for physical consequence and without fear, is what we were designed to do. We were made to jump in, get dirtied, be uncomfortable, get used up, risk survival, and go after the fullness of our lives.

The Cabin on the Hill

Friday, February 8: (20°F, low, clear; 36°F, high)

The interesting thing about such beautiful places is that they raise our aesthetic antennae and cause us to intently watch the visual signs. And in the midst of such staggering beauty, one sees distinctions more clearly between one little niche and another. In fact, it seems that beauty makes the eye more critical instead of less. "The whole Valley is gorgeous!" A true statement, indeed, but some places – some little micro-zones – are even *more* beautiful. It is an odd thing that once we find beauty, we start looking at how it is displayed and are able to experience differing arrays and degrees even in the midst of high pleasure.

On Thursdays we go for vegetarian pizza at The Hungry Bear in a small settlement, some 25 miles north of our cabin. It is extravagant, expensive, and somewhat wasteful to drive so far in the middle of the week to a lonely restaurant so many miles from the town where we are staying. To have come here to Montana so far away from where we belong– and yet we travel still further for a handful of vegetables on the most delicious bread I have ever eaten. This weekly journey has become a most sacred pilgrimage – we are like novitiates going into the Temple of Delights.

We likely would never have found The Hungry Bear, a taxidermist's dream of a bar – mammal heads everywhere peering over slot machines, a pool table, and a small diorama with a mountain lion - had we not stayed some seven years ago up in that area of the Valley where it is the only place to get a hot meal. Then, tired of our daily fare, we would go every Thursday night to get a vegetarian pizza, which seemed far more exotic in a place like this than bear and elk chili (which, by the way, is delicious). We chose Thursday randomly at that time, but Thursday nights have translated into special eat-out nights now even when we are at home. So the fact that it is a long drive to The Hungry Bear makes it most appealing, really.

But here, surrounded by two mountain cordilleras with stunning peaks like an exquisite double-beaded chain of pearls, I also experience a deeper and more melancholic beauty than I do down in the lower Valley where our town is. Up here the trees are much more closely spaced, the mix of species changes, and the road seems to narrow into a dark meandering trail through massive, high-spirited thickets packed with teaming long-haired epiphytes on towering evergreens and the double-sided backdrop of snowy summits on peak after peak. It is lonelier, far less inhabited, and wilder than the lower opening to the Valley where our town is located. And every time we go, I feel a deep, melancholic, compelling sadness that stirs me to realize that this is the deeper beauty, where valley is as exquisite as peak. We are no longer surrounded by beauty, but are actors inside the beautiful scene itself. And I always wonder, why does such deep aesthetic pleasure prompt such melancholia? Why, when we experience such complete visual ecstasy, do we match it with longing and sadness? Every Thursday I come back to the cabin longing for another place, even when I know this is a good-enough-gorgeousness here. Are we compelled to dissatisfaction as individuals or is it more that perfection humbles us when witnessed? Interestingly, it does not make our town less pretty – it makes that place up there more magical and turns it into an unfathomable thing, perhaps too much for daily fare. So Thursdays are days when I wake up increasingly thrilled as I anticipate the trip northward for a few hours to a place indescribably beautiful, where words fail and senses yearn.

Saturday, February 9: (26°F, low, partly cloudy; 41°F, high)

Whenever we come back to a place, we want it to be like our memory. We have considered this travel and have made plans based on known characteristics of where we are going. We are, in fact and deed, going back. We imagine how we will do things and where we will go and how it will be this second time around. We feel we have a better grip on life now that we can plan it out better. "This time, I know I want to go there every weekend and do that." So we come back with high hopes for an experience unlike any other in our daily lives – one whose trajectory is better known and better planned.

And what we find on the other side is life in its incessant movement of change, renewal, and decline. We find people with whom we have not stayed in contact but considered friendships-to-be-renewed, now ailing and some deceased. We find businesses we could not wait to visit, now closed up and bankrupt, and even more disturbing, we find new things everywhere – new people, new habits, and new histories – and we must encounter everything almost as if it were the first time. Some of it is exciting and brings bountiful gifts, and some of it is very sad, reminding us that "going home" is always and everywhere a euphemism.

Only a few weeks before we traveled here, one of the pioneers of this area passed away at 88. She was a founding member of the church and so we missed her greeting us that first Sunday morning. Her eager smile used to meet us across the sanctuary and draw us toward her as she sat with her violin beside the piano, ready for music to move the soul! She died right before we got to see her once more, and so we had to temper our delight at being reunited with people with their and our own sadness at missing someone so central to life in this place. She moved here more than 60 years ago from Florida and was an early settler in the southern part of the Valley. Her husband, who first worked as a "packer" leading hunting and fishing trips into the Bob Marshall Wilderness, died early, and she raised her eight children alone, teaching her family how to pray, hunt, fish, farm, and survive the vagaries of a monetized world, much in that same order. Today, her children and grandchildren, and great grandchildren, inhabit areas throughout this Valley and have become native Montanans. What steps we take re-aligns our descendants. History thinks forward, true Meaning emerges, and it uses us as pawns for a future we never get to see. We must trust it.

Making a Joyful Noise

Sunday, February 10: (21°F, low, wisp-like infrequent snow; 36°F, high)

It is strange to identify ourselves to others. And identity is always contextual. For the service providers and handymen we are "reverse snowbirds," for the lodges and gift shops we are out-and-out tourists, and for our neighbors and many townspeople we are friends-come-back. In our own heads we are explorers on a great journey not entirely unlike Lewis and Clark, as we walk in their steps and then forge some of our own. We are here to answer to a missing part of our lives – a need to be resourceful and self-sufficient.

Montana Winter Days

Yesterday we went to an art show in Bonner, a little sister settlement of Milltown, a former logging stronghold. The whole area now is sullenly quiet, almost death-like, with a large, closed mill and small, exquisite "no trespassing" tape on the old mill houses lining the road, each one slated to be torn down one-by-one as the land looks to slough off its history and now become an RV lot off I-90. It is all in a somewhat somnambulant state, somewhere between dead and pitifully resurrected. But the benefit that adheres to Bonner is that it is a short distance from Missoula, so it has a possibility of actually surviving "resurrection"; unfortunately, though, the past was likely its most beautiful state. There is a little K-8 elementary school in the town still thriving, though, and it is filled with artwork and exhibits for the community and tourists alike. In fact, you can pull off I-90 and come visit something here that is pure, hopeful, and future-oriented for us all. And in this school every year a group of artists celebrates the life, history, and works of a man who once headed the Art Department at the University of Montana and who came from this little settlement many years ago. It is sad and sweet and nostalgic and filled to the brim with life. Terms like decay, progress, and revitalization are trivial things in the face of deep soul and home-grown culture.

In the small gymnasium there were about 35 tables set up with the various types of artisans in this Guild – several were photographers, some watercolorists, some crocheters, one made lamps from old liquor bottles, one made lamps from tree trunks, several made bead jewelry, and one made wooden bowls. There was also a "fiber artist" who sold imported knitted gloves and scarves from Peru – that one left me pondering that perhaps those who gathered up useful items could be included as artists just for their talent in finding appropriate outer wear for the season. In the small library, student artwork was displayed everywhere and the Missoula Quiltworkers had draped their handicrafts over each side of the bookshelves, making a very intimate and beautiful quilt exhibit. And in the little cafeteria that could not hold more than 30 students even if you kept it at standing room only, four students were serving bean soup and a piece of bread for a warm lunch. It was their annual fundraiser.

What a savory taste of authentic Americana. A small town, challenged to survive at best, serving up the very deepest part of what it still is – hard-working, talented and inspired citizens who speak their voices in the most aesthetic ways. As we walked through the many exhibits surrounded by children's artwork, I wondered why our own schools in the East, many dripping fat and waste and complaining that they do not have funds to hire an art and music teacher, but who have white boards in every classroom, unused computer terminals sitting in long rows everywhere antiquating themselves every year, and Kindles stacked up throughout the reading rooms (as if books were some sort of archaic Rosetta Stone that could not possibly have any truths for right now in the present), could not learn from Bonner that needing to survive and struggling to be creative is the soul of confident, responsible, hard-working, and community-minded citizens.

I saw yesterday how many voices we all have, how many identities, but the greatest of these is hope for the future and appreciation for the past. I must remember to share this story with my uncle.

Montana Winter Days

Monday, February 11: (11°F, low, partly cloudy; 34°F, high)

Montana is a state of many contradictions and overlays. More than any other characteristic, this makes Montana sometimes funny. Most eating places are combo establishments, meaning they have a saloon, casino, and restaurant all in one. I don't know if this is to meet the needs of multiple types of clientele, make the establishment more adaptive to changing seasonal needs, or an accurate description of the various things a person would want to do on an outing in Montana at the same time.

It was in Montana in 2006 that my then-three year-old entered his first saloon as a way of traversing that part to get to the restaurant part. Now, on our second trip here, he is much more experienced with bars and saloons. At ten, he hails the friendly contemplatives nursing their drinks, and walks confidently through one area into another in assorted towns and establishments. He is also familiar with the unfriendly signs on most casino entrance areas (there are rarely doors) that say that "No One Under 18 Is Allowed Inside." They can stare into the place, watch the games, chat with the clientele, but they may not tread into that space. So yesterday after we had settled for a late lunch in a restaurant, my son said he had to go to the restroom and I told him to go on. He left the table and then came right back with eyes wide open: "Mom, the restroom is inside the casino and I'm not allowed in!" So accustomed to the way things are here that I no longer think there is anything strange about eating mid-way between liquor and slot machines, it took me a few seconds to understand the dilemma. Then I had to consider what we might do: do we break the law of nature or the law of society? Do we go outside and risk indecent exposure, not to mention frostbite, or do we march boldly into the unattended casino slot machine area and use the facilities anyway? After all, the only ones regulating any of the signs are a young, pregnant waitress, families with minors, and older men intently peering into frosted mugs. It first occurred to me to simply ignore the sign as an inconvenience.

Well, I mulled this over a minute and thought that it might not be a good idea to try to test my theory in front of my child, so I caught the pregnant waitress and asked her for some advice. She actually thought a minute, too, as if no minor had ever had to use the facilities there before or no one had ever actually read the signs, then she suggested that we go through the saloon and use their bathroom, because no one minded about that toilet. Well, besides opening another thought for me, I agreed that the saloon sign seemed less unfriendly, as we have often been in that area traveling through, so I sent him there. For some reason, a reason I cannot quite grasp, games of chance are far more corrupting than alcohol here. Now that I have learned this it may make facilities navigations much easier in the future.

A Very Montana Establishment

Tuesday, February 12: (26°F, low, sunny; 38°F, high)

It's funny – there are places hidden around here in somewhat plain sight. A few days ago we even heard that Prince William had visited one of the lodges down near Clearwater Junction. Being here every day does not mean that we have seen these places or know much about them, but over the last few weeks we have heard a few people talking about one of the lodges close to us and saying that their restaurant is very good and they have sleigh rides. So we drove up to see this place and encountered a very beautiful lodge that met all of the expectations of what a Montana mountain lodge "should be" according to the criteria of *Atlanta* magazine. Catering to tourists of every season including fly fishermen, big game hunters, snowmobilers, skiers, horseback riders, or simply those who want to have been here, it has a huge roaring fireplace, leather and wood everywhere, and low-lying massive rafters that make it seem like a perfect image of a large hospitable cabin in Montana. It is a well-crafted rugged look, as if Ralph Lauren had staged it perfectly with that groomed masculinity of the picturesque Wild West.

Everything is quiet and perfectly landscaped inside and out and you have an urge to sit down and simply "be" there. We "oo"-ed and "ah"-ed at the rustic, rugged, Western-y feel. Windows look out onto meadows where deer are scrubbing for growth in perfectly iced snowfields, looking as if they are tied in place and fed to stay exactly where they are. It is all very appealing and authentic in that Hollywood way. I expected Brad Pitt and Robert Redford to walk through at any moment chatting about fly fishing on the Blackfoot.

Then I came back to our cabin. At first I was a bit disoriented. It didn't look the same. But then I thought about our neighbors with their Confederate flag in the window, the humble logger who teaches us on Sundays, the shy pastor who trips over his words, the elementary school girls who played their hearts out in the basketball tournament this week, the school cook who eagerly told me about his healthy lunches, and the cake walk at the high school. And the $10.00 haircuts for all locals to raise donations for the family whose son drowned two weeks ago. And the lady who gave my son a pair of her personal ice skates that fit better than the ones he had and who insisted that we keep them and use them until we needed to pass them on. Oh, and the pregnant waitress who was very tired, but kindly ushered my son to the saloon restroom. And I realized that perhaps the word *authentic* has more meanings. Perhaps it has a meaning that is truer than our stereotyped images of the way things should be. I thought about the hard-working people, the quirky neighbors, the man who scrapes our drive on snowy days, and my son's school bus driver who always waves and says loudly, "Good Morning, Marjorie!" And then I looked back at our cabin and it looked like itself again. It made me smile to understand that word *authentic* a lot better now. We all seek what is authentic, but it is the stuff that creeps up around us as we live our normal lives, not what we imagine or see in someone else's life, that is really real.

Wednesday, February 13: (36°F, low, rain, snow and sleet; 38°F, high)

When we rented the cabin, there was already a renter in line, so today we had to move out to a hotel about a half-mile away and wait until the other inhabitants had their fun so that we could return. It is an awkward transaction, as almost four weeks have made us attached to our place and less amenable than we began. We kind of half-packed and then made three trips in the car to go the half-mile to the one hotel that is open in town. Since it was not quite worth packing seriously, that means we are surrounded by paper and plastic sacks, mis-matched items, and the debris of a partially-lived life. The car has items in disarray and the hotel room, with one bed for three people, two cats, and two dogs is challenging at best. We are living a far more rustic and rudimentary life here in the hotel than in the cabin. Instead of long glorious morning walks on the snow-covered logging road with our dogs, we are dodging trucks and snowplows in the hotel parking lot, begging our animals to quickly finish their business so that we can go back inside the cell to await liberation.

But having our lives temporarily stalled and interrupted is also a good experience. All of a sudden the little things that we worried about and troubled on in the cabin are diminished to insignificance. Suddenly, when we drive around town, we look enviously at people's houses where life occurs in a steady and more planned manner. And I have noticed that many of these very diverse places are cabins, even though they do not look at all alike. Some cabins are small, poorly insulated fishing houses, where summer people come to fly fish for trout on the rivers, some cabins are right in the middle of town, made of sundry materials, but compact and serviceable and housing townsfolk year-round, and other cabins are luxuriously constructed of huge ponderosa pines that mimic a settler's architectural plan but totally blown out of any reasonable proportion.

There is, in fact, a *real* cabin and a *real estate* cabin. They are not the same. One is humble and constructed of simple local materials to make a functional, efficient residence; it has minimal amenities and serves to shelter people. The other is built in the stereotypical image of a cabin but contains every urban commodity within. It is only partially built to shelter people: it also communicates a mood, loudly proclaims a status quo, and generates profit for the owner-landlords. Near here there is advertised a cabin for sale that has eight bedrooms, ten baths, two living rooms, a "chef's" kitchen, and a magnificent entranceway so that boarders can unload their outfits underneath a covered walkway in some of the most beautiful outdoors in America without actually making any type of physical contact with it. It is definitely not an efficient structure, either. Inside, there are some 5000 square feet of living space, windows galore, heavy made-to-appear-rustic furniture, and lovely iron-clawed standing tubs with heated floor tiles. It sits on 80 acres of prime meadowland that borders a famous fly-fishing river, and the price tag is $3.9 million.

In the News-eum in Washington, DC, they have the Unabomber's cabin on display. He lived and worked not too far from here. After arresting him, they literally picked up his cabin and carried it to Washington and put it inside a small room. But it doesn't look like that cabin for sale. And neither of them looks like the one in Dogtown which every minute we hope to return to soon. It leaves me to ponder, what does that word *cabin* really mean? I have to look that up in the dictionary when I get back. I must think about this some more.

Thursday, February 14: (26°F, low, snow; 40°F, high)

Today is Valentine's Day and so I woke my mother and son up earlier than I should, a not-too-difficult task in a communal bed, to give them each a box of "cowboy chocolates" that I had bought as a surprise in Missoula last weekend. I didn't know what they contained or what to expect, but the wooden boxes had COWBOY CHOCOLATES emblazoned on the top in capital letters and cattle brands burned along the top and sides of the boxes. When we opened them up, they were what we call in the East "boutique chocolates." Each was handmade, some colorfully wrapped in foils and some with surprise centers, but the general theme was huckleberry and cherry and nuts. Fresh and delicious, we each robbed more than one from the boxes before storing them inside the hotel dresser drawer away from the various and sundry animals in our room.

And the cats – not to be disturbed by our wayward antics and silly celebrations – have found a way to get literally under the boxed bed, literally inside it. They rest under there, unbothered by our issues, staying on cat time: night prowl, morning grub call, and then a long, undisturbed sleep under the bed. Everyone always says that cats are super-sensitive to place, but they are not sensitive to it in the same way that we are, as long as they can get solitude. I wonder why we are so sensitive to place. Why can't we get about the business of what we have to do in life and be less aware of where we do it? Hmm, there seems to be a lesson in this somewhere.

Cowboy Chocolates

Friday, February 15: (26°F, low, partly cloudy; 43°F, high)

Today we traveled to Kalispell, a rugged, dusty, frontier town that marks the western entrance to Glacier Park and the northern entrance to the Flathead Valley. It is a town of discrepancies and contradictions, where the wealthy pass through and the full-timers manage on a large degree of self-sufficiency and pluck, amused at the people who are stoned by the beauty around them. It is a town in a valley so fearsomely beautiful that it belittles you. I love this town. It has an extraordinary history tucked inside muddy streets, raunchy saloons, half-groomed sidewalks, and city planning that leaves you to wonder about the state of sobriety of those who put it together. Things grow up out of nowhere and roads wander willy-nilly crisscrossing each other and landing in strange roundabouts all of a sudden. Antique stores proliferate, selling wares that, in their tattered states, convey more about the true nature of the place than the current inhabitants. Kalispell is the living Wild West. No pretensions. Saloons, named various things like Silver Bullet, Montana Nugget, Moose's, Bandit, or Great Northern Bar dot the side streets along with ranch stores selling horse tack, feed of every type, and young livestock, and thrift stores that also stand in as food banks. Chain stores like Montana Wheat, which serves sandwiches, soup, and sweets to weary travelers all over the state, actually has the best bread and the sweetest pastries in its Kalispell store. Either the staff there is happier or they simply like to do things their own way, but Kalispell fare is one-of-a-kind, even in places where menus are fixed.

Seven years ago we passed through Kalispell very early one morning on the way to see the Kootenai River and the Yaak Valley way up in the northwestern corner of the state. I already loved the place, but that day we were just passing through and saw a little sign not more than three feet off the ground and pushed firmly down in the snow and mud that said, "Event Today at the Fairgrounds." We went on to the Yaak, made our way up some pretty treacherous roads on snow and ice, had a makeshift lunch in a bar where not only were we the sole clients during the lunch period, but we were looked at as if we were a new and unknown species, and then started back, had ice cream at the Dairy Queen in Libby, visited their Chamber of Commerce, and then traced our steps backward to Kalispell, where I remembered that sign and so headed to the Fairgrounds to see what was left of the Event.

Around the largest building on the fair grounds were a few cars, so we parked near that building and went inside to find rows of tables, maybe 25 vendors with their artwork, handcrafts, and baked goods for sale. It was small overall and in the back area near the restrooms there was a small space with a stool and two petite risers pointed inward to look like a stage of some sort. At most it could aspire to hold 10-15 people. As far as visitors and potential customers, however, I doubt there were more than seven of us in the venue at that time, three of those my own family. We made our way through the sales area somewhat uncomfortably, feeling like deer in the crosshairs for vendors who appeared to have had few customers all day and who dreaded packing up all the stuff they didn't sell. But then about halfway through the rows, we heard a guitar strumming and a rough, strangely melodic croon coming from the stage area. We headed over, not more than 20 feet away, and found a couple of forlorn vendors, who had obviously already given up on us and were sitting on the bleachers drinking coffee, and a curly, red-headed man with a huge cowboy hat, vest, boots, and spurs perched on the stool singing, *"John Wesley Hardin, shot a man for snorin', shot him in the bed, right where he lay."* I stopped abruptly, momentarily considering these pithy lines, and the red-headed man smiled warmly at us and motioned with his head for us to sit down and join "them" (meaning his wife and the two vendors). Not knowing what else to do, we sat down for a 30-minute show, where we got more eye contact than we would from a near-sighted optometrist. Each song a Western ballad of dire straits, whether about barroom brawls, cheatin' women, ornery cattle, or sleep-deprived outlaws, was so compelling that it required thoughtful consideration to follow the lyrics and it conjured up very vivid images of Western life. And the guitar player sang many songs during those 30 minutes.

We stayed until the set ended, and then thanked the rough, red-headed cowboy singer, who quickly put his guitar down and shook our hands firmly and warmly saying, "My name is Badwater Bill, and it is nice to meet you!" Again, I was momentarily stalled in my thinking – what kind of name is "Badwater Bill"? So I asked him, "Where did you get a name like that?" He smiled proudly, as if he had waited a lifetime for this question, and he told us his story. He came to Montana from Maryland, where he had had enough of "that life" and wanted "this life" instead. He taught himself to play guitar, rounded up every great Western ballad he could find (and some that weren't so great), practiced playing and singing hour after hour, and was eventually hired as entertainment for tourists who go on evening horseback trails with a chuck wagon at a local Kalispell ranch. With his smiling wife beside him offering to sell us his one-and-only CD (which we enthusiastically purchased), I found myself strangely in awe of this converted Easterner who had the guts to live out his dream.

As we traveled over the next few weeks, my then-three year-old son memorized the lyrics to every outlaw shooting, barroom brawl song on the CD and we never forgot about

Badwater Bill. I tried to find out once if he had any more CDs, but I could never locate him. If I could, though, I'd like to tell him that I remember him so much and that his smile and songs for me are ubiquitous with the town of Kalispell and the feel of the genuine West; after all, West is what comes out from inside, not a birthplace on some certificate at the county courthouse. Badwater Bill was no pretender; he was the genuine, bona fide real thing.

    Why this reminiscence? Tonight a rowdy rodeo is coming to Kalispell with bull-riding finals, so I expect the locals will begin pouring in as the hour nears and the restaurant-saloon-casinos will be hopping. Kalispell will come alive tonight and live up to its true nature, I imagine. I wish I could be there. Somehow, though, now-ten-year-olds are more morally delicate than three year-olds. I guess I'll stay away this time.

Rodeo in Kalispell

Saturday, February 16: (20°F, low, sunny; 42°F, high)

Yesterday my son attended a birthday party. Well, that is what I am calling it, because the event was provoked by commemoration of a birthdate of his new friend eleven years ago. But it was not like any birthday party I had ever been to.

It was planned as a spend-the-night birthday party at the boy's house. The GI Joe invitations were very creative and informed the guests to bring their boots, snowsuits, and a sleeping bag, and, oh, yes, "remember to wear your camouflage." Well, I really should back up a bit…my son told me that the little boy's real birthday was during the December school holidays but that the family had decided on February 15th as the best celebration day. I have to admit that from this point on I was mystified, wondering how many birthdays a person can legitimately have.

All of the 5th grade boys were invited to the party, and all but one said they were attending. So we went to Missoula and purchased a packet of University-logoed notebooks, pens, and sundry other paraphernalia thinking this would be a great gift for a local boy at that age, as "The Griz" are very popular here. My son agreed it was a "neat" gift and so I drove him off to the birthday boy's house, several miles off the main road. My plan was to drop off my son for an hour or so and then pick him up, as I could not imagine the need for a sleepover nor could I fathom what winter camping meant as a concept. So off we went with snowsuit, boots, and University-themed gift.

The little boy's house was quite nice, nestled in the trees on the side of a very steep depression that was surely a beautiful meadow in the summertime, and when we pulled up there were four boys already playing in the snow (although when I looked closely I noticed they were actually at the outdoor faucet washing something in running water while standing in at least

10 inches of snow). I quickly instructed my own child to stay out of the water and be ready to leave in an hour and a half when I drove by. In fact, I gave him my watch so that he knew the time and would be as mindful as I could expect from a 10 year-old boy. I thought that he could live through just about anything for 90 minutes, so I drove away. After all, we were here for the authentic Montana experience, so I figured we all may as well dive in. My son was enthusiastic and seemed awfully eager for me to get the car fully turned around and heading out. Just as I turned right out of their driveway, I saw a figure that looked awfully familiar to me lunge toward the running spigot.

    I went on, did some errands, and then returned, picked up my son, and began to hear the story of what he described as "the most wonderful birthday party ever!" In his sodden snow boots, scooping out ice and snow from his feet and around his ankles onto the car floormat, he told me that this was a Winter Camp Survival Birthday Party. When we first arrived, he said, the boys had already started gathering roots for their dinner and that is what they were washing at the outdoor faucet when he got there unfashionably late. Intrigued, amazed, and stunned, I asked which roots they had gathered and he told me, "My friend said that we could eat any roots in order to survive, so we pulled up anything we could find." Then they went down into the meadow area behind the house, where the snow had to be much deeper than 10 inches, and set up tents for the camping, aided by the little boy's father. When I arrived, they had just finished starting a "huge bonfire," as my son described it, and they had just put the roots into a pot and begun cooking them.

    By this time in the tale, my lower jaw had disconnected with amazement, and I had to remind myself to be quiet to hear the story. My son, who did not know what camouflage was and didn't own any anyway and so was dressed in jeans and a nice Western-buttoned shirt and sweater for the event, then removed a bottle of water from his jacket and told me that they had given him his own "canteen," as he was woefully unprepared for the party. On the plastic water bottle were camouflage tape strips supposedly to disguise the bottle label that read "crystal clear mountain water." He said he really had needed a canteen, even in the cold snow, because they had been playing Capture the Flag and were chasing and tackling each other all over the woods, calling out on walkie talkies to locate the enemy, before stopping to set up their "Winter Camp." Those words had initially prompted this beautiful vision of the Lakota Indians in *Dances with Wolves*, with their scenic-tragic Winter Camp in the mountains. I could soothingly hear Kevin Costner's voice as he made his way closer and closer. But then my son's voice intruded again and I envisioned those young camouflaged boys running around a tent, in and out of the woods, hollering commands while unidentified roots boiled on the fire for dinner, and my mood shifted abruptly.

Actually, when I picked him up, I had interrupted a conversation between the little boy's mother and father. She was asking the father if he was prepared in case a bear attacked them that night, and he scoffed at her, saying, "there are no bears out in the middle of winter!" as if her worries were the most ridiculous female irrationality he had ever heard. He then added, "I am only concerned about lions and there aren't many of them around. They should leave us alone tonight because of the deep snows." Two thoughts crossed my mind simultaneously: I wondered how many mountain lions it would take to eat so many little boys and what reasonable winter animal would walk down into that meadow with snow drifts everywhere to attack frozen, hollering boys? I silently agreed with the father that aside from the sub-zero temperatures and ill-prepared survivalists, other external threats were probably quite low.

Since hearing the rest of this story from my son, though, I have had occasion to think a bit, and I must admit some things to myself – this is a very creative party theme; it definitely teaches lessons (although I am not sure of either the content or outcome of those); it engages the creative and explorative nature of this aged child; it helps the boys get to know more about the environment and to appreciate it and respect it for various reasons; it is a fount of proto-scientific lessons of trial-and-error, including the unfortunate botanical possibility of learning what is a bad root choice; and it sure as heck beats playing video games and sitting in the house. On retrospect, I am glad my son had this experience and a little part of me, too, thought it was a really "neat" idea, even though some cognitive dissonance remains between these concepts of birthday party and winter camp.

I did later learn that the party boy's parents had hot dogs as a back-up menu item in case the roots didn't work out and had cleared out a space in the basement in case the less-seasoned boys could not make it through the night. At least that is what the survivors reported on Monday at school. One of them had run off during the night and returned to his own heated house and down comforter prompting his mother to call the party boy's totally surprised mother in the dead of the night and report that he had made it home safely. I guess the lesson I most take from all of this is that if you have a birthday party sleepover, you better lock them inside the tent or house first.

Marjorie M. Snipes

The Winter Birthday Camp

Sunday, February 17: (26°F, low, heavy morning snow; 36°F, high)

I love the life and people out here precisely because they are different, but they incorporate the same levels of contradiction and intellectual incongruity that we do in the East. Away from cities like Missoula, with its university and social commerce with large amounts of diverse people and ideas, there is a prevailing and customary local mentality that is interesting to me because it is complex and layered. On one hand, when locals go out to get their mail from the post office or run to the little Valley market to grab something quickly, they very, very often leave their cars running, keys in the ignition. Those who do not practice this do practice leaving the doors unlocked on cars and, as many have told us, on houses, too. In the library, people leave their packages, pocketbooks, and bookbags to use the computer or look for a book or have a conversation with someone across the room. In diners, patrons use the restroom and leave their things at the table. During social events, whether a basketball game or a book reading, people leave their accoutrements behind as place holders on their seats while they go for concessions, a bathroom break, or a casual conversation across the gymnasium. And while ice skating, people mound up their things, including wallets, on the bench at the far end of the pond and skate about, never looking back to the area. There is a prevailing attitude of trust and reliability in social situations, a generally relaxed attitude.

But that is not the whole story. It happens that right now, because of the "last-straw" atrocities at Sandy Hook Elementary and all the many killings that have occurred just within the last few months in our country, there is a very lively and argumentative dialogue going on nationally about gun control. Here, this conversation is front and center in a way it was not in my hometown in Georgia. Everywhere I go I hear snippets of heated discussion, not debate, just affirming discussion that this type of legislation is very bad and is threatening to the people who live here. Today, after a conversation in church about our duties as Christians to follow God's law and those laws of society that are not immoral, even if we disagree with them, one very upstanding member of the group spoke out about this legislation saying that he believed the proposed gun laws were not moral because he had the God-given and Constitution-given right to protect his family at any cost. He then stated, "I would die to defend this."

At first, I reacted as if this was said for social impact and chuckled at the serious tone, but then I saw how intent he was in his convictions. This is a man whom I greatly admire for his integrity, wisdom, devotion, and leadership, but in that moment, I saw him as flawed as I am. I wondered about two different things: why would someone who so firmly believes in a God-centered and –directed life feel that he needed to take ownership over such a sovereign level of protection? And what was so threatening to him that he was emotionally dislodged to respond in such an assertive manner? After all, he was not threatened by high levels of crime and degradation in and around his neighborhood as I am in the East. In fact, he lives several miles from town on large acreage with one of the most beautiful rivers in the world, where his greatest threat is a grizzly bear or coyote or wildfire or naïve poacher looking for the first big trophy head of his life. He went on to argue that the government was increasingly acting tyrannical by taking away liberty after liberty that had been fought for by our forefathers who submitted to God in a way that these current politicians would not recognize.

I understood the argument. I understand the argument, but I don't see the line that has supposedly been breached. It would seem to me that there would be a reasonable number of weapons that anyone could actually wield and that it would be reasonable that no private citizen alone amass an arsenal in his own home. To me, the idea of citizen democracy and constitutional right is that the government is beholden to the People, not to a person. That plurality is the crux of the matter. In my mind this one man (or any one person) would not need then dozens of weapons because he could not use dozens of weapons at any one time. Instead, his rhetoric and conviction should be his greatest weapon stockpile, just like our forefathers.

But the other part of the conundrum for me was the high sense of imminent threat. This prompted me to my own confused thinking: I am living right now in an area where no one seems to sense any danger from others, thereby leaving their things and their persons very exposed and vulnerable in a way that I certainly do not practice in my own neighborhood back home. Instead, they feel threatened by a faceless and really nameless external "thing," while in Georgia I live concerned about neighbors two doors down and a crime spree occurring in my home neighborhood right now. They are hunters, but also see their weapons as ways to protect themselves, whereas I live exposed and without weapons, my only protection a thin piece of metal on my door at night which only serves to lock me out from time to time when I forget my key.

As an anthropologist, I can look at this and analyze it in multiple ways arguing that because they are small and thinly populated, the largesse of the "outside" is indeed threatening, but then I also think back to more interesting ideas including the rather constant self-awareness that they are a favored people living in an exquisite and deeply desired geographical area, where outsiders come in and want to purchase and gobble up paradise in what appears to them a vulgar and greedy manner. Among the working class local homes and businesses, there are scattered affluent rental homes and summer fishing cabins, one of them currently occupied by me. I can see that year-long residents might not just sense, but actually experience, transient colonization by outsiders who do not understand daily life for people living in and off of place. I can see that they feel need to protect their lives from unsought changes of all kinds, whereas I come from an area where change is as regular as morning coffee, where argument is the primary basis of conversation, and where rubbing up against diversity is common, expected, and oddly comforting.

I cannot say that one is right and one is wrong. I go back to the beginning. I am here precisely because they are different. I am here for revitalization precisely because my own life back home has fatigued me. I am here to seek that idealism and delight at feeling that I live in the midst of something original and primordial here. I am drawn to understanding these complexities and contradictions because they allow me to transcend my own narrow ways of thinking. No, one is not right and one is not wrong. They are different. They are authentic pieces of the human heart and mind. But as I left the church service today, there was a group of men huddled at the door talking urgently and they quieted as I approached. I laughed aloud and told them it looked as if they were in the midst of a conspiracy. Then, the oldest one stepped forward and shook my hand and told me that he hoped I had a good week and everyone else smiled. Socially adept when necessary, they dispensed with me courteously. That is the rest of the story, but I know that is not the whole story.

Monday, February 18: (29°F, low, mostly sunny; 41°F, high)

There are some things out here that I find very interesting: on the one hand some people put up a "House for Sale" or "Business for Sale" sign and just leave it there while they go on about their lives. We met a lady living right on the Blackfoot River with a small in-house business of new cloth and quilts, used items and books scattered in and among stuff. On the sign outside her house it says, "Quilt 4 Sale; Shop for

Sale; 2Hand Items; Details Inside" and then a big "OPEN" sign on the door. We stopped and went in, bought a few small things, and then talked with her. I asked her if she was moving, and she said she didn't know. I asked her if the sign meant she was selling her business, and she said she didn't know. I then asked her more directly what the sign meant. She told us she was in her 70s and wanted to retire sometime. She said she put up the sign because she was open for any offers anyone had – "if they offer me enough, I will let them have it and I will move."

That is very sage advice. I think when I go back home I will put up a sign in my yard; after all, if someone offered me "enough," I would move, too.

On the other hand some people have businesses that are unadvertised and yet they expect customers to show up. When we were here before, there was a man in the Valley who had a sign out advertising "Antiques." We never forgot the shop because it was really a series of shops, nothing heated, dirt and iced floors, and antiques and collectibles stuffed so tightly in every crevice that you could stand in one place (usually on ice) for literally thirty minutes and still not get an accurate inventory. I purchased a few little things from one corner of one shelf and did not even consider looking anywhere else. It was too much. Knowing the southeastern corner of one part of the shed seemed sufficient at the time.

But this time we could not find his house and shops. We looked and looked and then started methodically scouting him out. We asked at The Hungry Bear if he was still in the area and they said, "Yes." So, with high hopes we mentally divided the highway into grid points like forensic archaeologists and thoroughly searched until we spied what we believed to be the most likely geographical candidate. There was no sign, but we had a "vague feeling about the area." I parked on the side of the highway and walked his driveway (which was long) almost up to the front door. (Why I didn't drive my car in I don't know – I guess I thought a walking person was less threatening, albeit far more bizarre, in freezing temperatures.) All around us was cleared property and one large barn. But we had remembered lots of trailers and outbuildings when we were there before, so I remained a bit skeptical about the "feeling."

I had almost gotten to his front steps when the door opened, confirming what I always think about people: most people keep an eye on the front yard area and "stay in the know" about everyone else. (At least I know my neighbors do this in Georgia and, when I am home, I do, too.) So the elderly man came out and along with him bounded a young black Lab barking vigorously. I hollered up to ask him if he was the man who had the antiques and he answered, "Let me get my keys!" I wasn't entirely sure what kind of answer this was, but I walked back towards the middle of the drive and waited. He put on his coat and came to join me. I then re-asked if he still had the antiques store because we remembered a sign here about seven years ago. He said that he did have an antiques store but that he had taken down his sign many years ago because not many people ever came anymore. Now this troubled me – how can you ever hope to have customers if you take down your free in-your-own-yard advertisement and just wait on people to find you some other way?

He opened the door to the barn and proudly showed us his antiques, telling us that he had sold a lot of them and now had much less than he used to. This was true. He had much less than before - some boxes, old washing machines, milk cans, tools, and used gas pumps. I apologized for bothering him, and he smiled heartily and said, "No need to apologize. This is what my customers do; they all just come up and knock on the door." I asked about the outbuildings I remembered and he said that he used to have a lot of old trailers he rented out to loggers, but that the economic downturn and rising unemployment had left fewer people needing housing and so he had just hauled them all off. "Well, it sure doesn't look like the same place," I told him, and he agreed.

We bought a few things from him and he said he'd walk us back to the car so that he could get his mail. We waved goodbye with him telling us that we were always welcome to come by and buy some of his stuff anytime we wanted. I felt like a 'shine runner during Prohibition Days, able to sniff out likely marketplaces of under-the-counter merchandise. Perhaps I should consider my own house and contents a business and not advertise and just see if anyone will offer me something for my stuff?

Tuesday, February 19: (22°F, low, partly cloudy; 45°F, high)

At the post office today, a place where the town convenes to share gossip, check on upcoming events, and greet friends on a daily basis, there was a car parked beside me with two elderly women. The older of the two, probably in her early 80s, got out by herself with four large, bulky packages while the other sat in the driver's seat with the motor idling. I offered to help her with the packages, but she smiled and said, "I can carry them – thank you." So I went ahead of her and opened the post office door for her, conditioned by my upbringing to never take "no" for an answer when I still see a way to help. So she went ahead of me and plopped her packages on the countertop inside the post office. One by one, the postmistress weighed, measured, and tallied up the costs, the lady paid, and she left.

I mailed my envelope and headed back to the car. By this time the younger of the old ladies had the car backed up and was beginning to move forward, and I couldn't help but see the rear of the vehicle. On the back windshield was a large sticker covering about one third of the glass which said, "Got my horse, got my dog; don't need no cowboy."

I don't have anything else to add; I just thought that was something to think about.

Women at the Post Office

Wednesday, February 20: (23°F, low, snow, then sunny and windy; 39°F, high)

The other day I went to the local veterinarian. She works half time and has a receptionist to help her. No vet techs, no janitors, no staff except the receptionist that day. The office is small and has a tiny icy parking lot out in front where the lives of both clients and owners alike are under imminent threat, so I entered with some trepidation to see when she could do a check-up of my dog who suffered breast cancer a few months ago. When I went in during the morning, there were no other cars in the parking lot; however, the receptionist said the vet was booked. Then she considered her statement again, somewhat wistfully, and said, "Now there may have been a cancellation today – let me check." She walked back into the back and I heard talking and then she came up front and said, "Yes, we've had a cancellation and you can come this afternoon at 2:00."

At 2:00 I returned with my dog's shot record and papers from our home vet and saw a different woman at the desk. She was very friendly and looked at the shot record and asked if I was originally from Kalispell. You see, my dog's name is Kalispell. In Georgia, they have no idea what this word is and, in fact, rarely understand what I am saying. My brother-in-law still thinks her name is "Cow's Bell" and often states that I chose a very odd name for a dog and he is glad I never named any of their pets. In Montana, though, this name conjures up all sorts of unknowable associations, I'm sure, but I chose the name because I like the town of Kalispell and think it is a great name. In fact, if I get another dog I intend to name her Miss Oula.

Well, I told the lady at the desk that I was not from Kalispell but from Georgia, no need to give her a specific hometown name, as all places in some place that far away would be considered pretty much alike. She looked at my dog, which is a borzoi, and back at me and asked if the dog was from Kalispell. "No," I said, "none of us is from there. We are all pretty much from Georgia, give or take a few miles here and there." She acted relieved suddenly and chuckled, and said, "Well, I thought it was strange for a minute because I knew there were no borzoi breeders or owners in Kalispell." Now this left me thinking again – I had never thought that names were so important. Perhaps I have been going about naming too indiscriminately. Perhaps people in Kalispell, Montana would be insulted to know that my dog is named after their town. I had never thought about this before. She then went on to say that this was the first borzoi she had seen in her practice, that borzois had "fallen out of favor" among the general populace.

Wishing to change the conversation, I asked her if I would have to wait a while on the vet or if they were running on schedule and she laughed and said, "Well, here I am!" Confused, I looked at her more closely and saw she had on a name tag with the title "Dr." We both laughed, although I bet we were laughing at two different things. She said that they were rarely very busy and then told me that the parking lot sometimes would be filled with cars, even blocking the small road, and that sometimes the waiting area was filled with people, and no animals were anywhere among any of them. She said sometimes she would have a dog in the back and come out and find lots and lots of people crowding in because they recognized someone's vehicle in the parking lot and wanted to stop and talk a while or find out what was wrong with Mr. Jones's dog. She also said that she sometimes has people come in and shut the door and ask her about some kind of human ailment or weird rash. She cautioned me to never think things are what they seem at first. Now I expect that is some wise advice, since I would agree with her now that I have lived here a while. Meanwhile, I was increasingly uncomfortable, wondering what kind of establishment *this* was – if restaurants are also saloons and casinos, and elementary school cafeterias are multi-purpose rooms with pianos, rock walls, and ski equipment storage and changing areas, then maybe veterinarians are something else as well?

    I don't have much of a story here except to say that I enjoyed meeting her, found her bright, devoted, and extremely helpful and hopeful about my Kalispell. She talked more than half an hour, recommended a sonogram every six months, a stick-to-it faith and rugged hope that there would be no recurrence, the consideration of chemotherapy tablets if the worst occurred, and then she heard a loud "meow!" from the parking lot and said, "Well, my next friend is here!" She charged me $18. for the visit and left me considering how beautiful small-town life truly can be, where people only need to earn what they need, always stay in touch with local news, and care about each other on a first-name basis, regardless, alas, of what that first name is.

Marjorie M. Snipes

The Vet and Her Best Friends

Thursday, February 21: (17°F low, sunny; 32°F, high)

The season is changing, but it does so almost – but not quite – imperceptibly. Several days go by and I notice "no change," but then, all of a sudden, I realize that we are waiting for the bus in the morning in an early sunshine and the dusk has passed. I walk the dog and make note that I can see little holes in the snow where mud is forming, areas we must avoid to keep floors clean inside. And in the evening, when my body longs to sleep with the sun, I find that the clock is running later than I thought.

It is beautiful to make note of the seasons and to spend time considering change in all its states. I often think that I would embrace change more positively throughout my life if I had a chance to consider it before the shift occurred. Whether something as cyclical as seasons and the earth's rotation, in which I either too-eagerly await the shift or mourn the passing of a beautiful season long before it actually occurs, or something as irrevocable as aging, in which I experience both beauty and sadness at watching my child grow into young adolescence and away from the dearest closeness of childhood, and at watching my own self move steadily along an unknowable path toward completion, I seem to always be trying to catch up to the things that happen instead of waiting, watching, and embracing them. I hear someone say, "This is a lack of faith for the future, lack of trust," but I know that it is much more complex than that. We do not live only in minds – our own bodies change, whether seasonally or longitudinally, and require us to reconsider and readjust yet again. I struggle with the fact that I do find joy in almost every change, but I find it slowly, after I have had time to consider it, experience it many times, and grow into it. Then I make my way around it slowly and begin to count on it being there. I figure out a way to live with it well. Then, it goes away, I begin to mourn it, and something else forces my attention.

I expect that the secret to this all is to either find joy quickly or to live in joy. Both of those are nice sayings and nice ideas. They would make a good sermon. But, as for me, it is not as simple as saying that is the right path. I still face each day confident, hopeful, only to find that something else has changed on me again. I get distracted by it, sometimes anxious about it, sometimes frustrated and angry, sometimes joyful – some changes are good things - but nothing stays put in life. Nothing at all. Not even the snow in our front yard and the beautiful winter.

All this constant movement inside and out. When I am quiet, I am sometimes afraid to acknowledge how little control and authorship I have over anything at all.

Friday, February 22: (24°F, low, heavy snow; 36°F, high)

There is that story about the Eskimos and their multitudinous words for "snow." Coming from Georgia, I find that an interesting story because of my own lack of imagination. Let's see…we have snow, sleet, hail, frost, ice – oh, and "rabbit ice," too. That's all. Nothing else comes out of a cold sky. When we need more ways of expressing it, we start using adjectives, "slushy snow," "wet snow," "dry snow," "icy snow," "hard snow," "soft snow." I bet those are not official terms anywhere but in the South.

But here, there is stuff coming most days and I keep saying "it is snowing," but one day is not like another. Some days it is soft and lacy, some days big and heavy, some days sharp and stinging, and some days well-nigh invisible. And there are other varieties as well. Truth is, I don't know what to call it to distinguish it, but since I am usually reporting the weather to other Southerners living with me, "It's snowing!" seems to do the trick just fine.

In school at the beginning, my son was confused and disappointed when the students did not get excited about the outside weather; he would come home and say "It snowed all day and nobody seemed to notice!" This was a moral dilemma for him, since snow means excitement and imminent school release in the South. He sat there all day, watching it snow, expectantly waiting for them to announce that school was closing, and no one paid any attention to what was happening. This made quite an impression on him.

Yesterday morning I walked the dog a long time. It was one of those warm-ish mornings when being outside trumps anything else imaginable and just walking in large circles is satisfying to the soul. The snow was very iced up and crunchy, as we have had warm afternoons for several days and it melts and then re-freezes. It still looks opaque, but every footstep teeters and slides ever-so-slightly in the mornings and then sinks and slips around in the accumulation by afternoon. It makes walking similar to being on a beach in the afternoon, each step leaving a mold and indentations that anyone can follow. We follow the deer footsteps in the afternoon and they follow ours after we leave. But in the mornings, we walk as if traversing the South Col of Everest, trying to stay in the path lines and not step onto a small ridge that unbalances us and leaves our muscles tweaking and twitching.

The dog has taken to walking on the mounds of snow beside the path, as they are less beaten down and easier to traverse. But I cannot walk there because air pockets have formed in sneaky places and sometimes when I walk on the banks, I sink up over my thighs and fall back softly on my behind. It always leaves me laughing, but one dose produces a sufficient adrenaline rush. On the logging road, it is nice after the snowmobiles have their fun because they leave us nice tracks to follow. I must wait on them this morning.

The Logging Road

Saturday, February 23: (30°F, low, light snow; 34°F, high)

Smell can incite the imagination in powerful ways....

Montana is a very manly place, a terribly sexist statement if I ever heard one. But when looking at the contrast between life in the East and life in Montana, there is quite a bit of room for stereotypes. Fishing, hunting, bulky winter gear, guns and knives, rustic log cabins, snow scrapers, tire chains, and saloons, snowmobiles at breakneck speed, leatherworks, and tracking. Women can do all of these things, and I know women in Montana who do all of these things, including taxidermy, but in my stereotyped Eastern mind, I live in a very masculine place.

And around the cabin where I live, there is a whole host of beautiful men whose presence I detect in my mind through my nose! They wear natural fibers and they have that rugged, rustic, manly smell like Old Spice. They are all hard workers, constantly molding and shaping the world into something that has their mark distinctly stamped upon it, something that says, "Halt, I go here and this is all mine - people, animals, and land." Every morning when I walk outside I feel almost withered with desire, as I look around me and experience their presence.

Our cabin sits in its own world and sometimes acts defiantly as if it were the only thing that exists. Snow whorls make neighbors disappear, a large, foreboding hill, almost 25 feet tall blocks off the backside, and a small lake, permanently frozen, stares at me frontside. Ponderosa and lodgepole pines scattered willy-nilly, some gnarled and gasping for life from rather incessant deer rubbings that grind them down daily, block out sundry other signs of company. It is just us, the deer, the snow, the hill, the lake, the trees, and the many men of my imagination.

Between the tall hill and the cabin, though, there is a logging road wide enough for a single vehicle, but except for an occasional dog on a leash, a straggler passing through, the pastor's daughter's horse, or weekend snowmobiles, the road sits covered in ice and snow like a Robert Frost diorama, saying "which way will I go? Right or left?" Every morning I cannot wait to get to this road, some 20 yards from our cabin door, to walk the dog, to just be alone, or to be with the men whom I sense there most mornings – lots and lots of them.

The hill and the road extend for a long way, far more than two miles if you were to be so inclined as to measure it.

And on the other side of the hill there is usually a lot of noise except for Sundays. The lumber company, like a gigantic lorax factory on the other side, has saws shearing boards, kilns boiling continually to dry the wood and whining brakes of logging trucks coming in and out of the work area bringing incessant offerings. This makes up the soundscape of our lives. It is like "white noise," though, because a single birdsong will pierce it and cause everyone to look. As far as the pictoscape, we see little besides snow, trees, a hill, a frozen lake, and occasionally the Confederate flag in our friendly neighbor's window. In fact, the only pictogram the logging company gives us is a single or double stack of steam boiling upward toward the sky in the near distance. The sights and sounds of the logging company are relatively, overall, unobtrusive. But the smell is not unobtrusive. I guess that would be an aromascape. The smell is ubiquitous. It is fragrant, piercing, and gut-wrenching. Had I not missed our road the first day and seen the logging company on the other side of the hill, I would have reported that we have a very large Old Spice company right behind us, making gallons and gallons of daily brew to incite and inspire women everywhere.

But, alas, it is not an Old Spice factory. It is a logging company. It does make me wonder, though, why the trees dress up so well and use so much aftershave to go to their funerals. I do not think of the corpse-like trees when I am walking on the logging road or sitting outside – because of the smell, I only think about the men wearing that pungent, tickling fragrance. They are everywhere in my life here, crowding all my senses except the eyes.

Montana Winter Days

Man in a Jar

Sunday, February 24: (17°F, low, partly cloudy, then sunny; 38°F, high)

Yesterday we went to Missoula early in the morning for piano lessons. On the way out we passed car after truck after camper tracing our steps backwards to go into our town for the SnowJoke Half Marathon, a run, sprint, walk, trudge, skate, teeter, lumber around the lake from start to finish. The "joke" is that the weather means it is anyone's guess as to what the day will be like, and yesterday there were some four inches of new-fallen snow on top of some ten inches of old stuff all over the Race Course - a partially paved road wandering around the lake and through the woods. We heard from the locals that people went about their business of traversing the area in snow boots, tutus, angels' wings, red long johns, or whatever accoutrements helped them not freeze or break their necks and to laugh. The local paper said there were 600 entrants this year, almost half the size of the town itself. As we traveled southwest, we were thinking that maybe, just maybe, Missoula would be half-emptied itself today.

But, alas, such a paltry number of people makes no difference to the mighty Missoula, so we entered the city dodging cars, pedestrians, and haphazardly-placed stop signs and red lights as usual. Missoula is fascinating because it wears its history as an outer garment of life. As we made our way into the downtown area we passed the usual bars, grills, casinos, and saloons, all in their original shells, feeling as accustomed to them as we are to diners and churches in Georgia. I guess in one place you eat and pray and in the other you drink and pray. But, then, something else caught my eye. Right off Orange Street, there was a hair salon that had emblazoned in the front window a glaring neon sign that said, "Hair Salon and Shampoo Bar." As with most things in life that juxtapose contradictory images,

I had to stop and think, this time about a salon saloon or a beauty bar. What fun! I slowed down the vehicle to take a second look, causing the man behind me to start scanning the street for wildlife, of the human or animal variety. (That is the only reason you slow down in Montana.) And I glared again, thinking that maybe I had misread it. But I hadn't. As with most things, the first shot was the most accurate.

So we continued on after the short mental detour and made our way to the piano teacher's house. Over the weeks we have grown to love this ritual and enjoy our hour-and-a-half at his house. He teaches piano as if it were a finely-choreographed dance between the body and the instrument, each note a separate arrangement of the hips, legs, feet, shoulders, arms, wrists, and, oh, the fingers! In fact, the fingers do not exist at all – they are multiple phalanges, each with its own calling, and every finger pad has an owner's manual all to itself. My son sits down, plays Bach *Prelude in C minor* and then for the next 84 minutes the teacher prods, pulls, re-arranges, and stacks my child's body this way and that so that when he plays it again, it sounds as if angels were crooning their melancholic notes to the strums of heavenly lyres.

My son has studied piano for several years and this is his fourth teacher. The first one inspired us like a heavenly angel, for the first time in my life showing me how expressive and emotive the piano could be, but then he started making music elsewhere as well and ran off with a woman who was not his wife and deserted everyone, us included. We mourned that one for a while, but then we found a second one. She was a brilliant teacher of mechanics and techniques, a teacher's teacher, and because of her giftedness he learned what she had to teach, and then he was ready for "repertoire," that time when you learn through a somewhat more Socratic method, playing songs of staged difficulty and being corrected endlessly on every move and every sound, where nothing is good enough anymore. So we then switched to a college-level teacher, who had agreed to listen to my son and make a teacher recommendation among her peers, but when she heard him play she said, "I will take him, but be warned: I do not teach children and may not know how to speak to him on his age level." (He was nine at the time.) We never had to worry about this, though, because they speak piano to each other and have no problems communicating. But when we decided to come to Montana, I had to make a temporary arrangement, and so I found the fourth piano teacher in Missoula through a process that can only be described as intuitive searching, like taking a dowsing rod out in the backyard and waiting for it to tremble.

I love watching the alchemy of the piano lesson. It can only be described as magic. Sometimes a spell is cast and it transforms everything and makes life beautiful, and sometimes the mixing results in a "ca-boom!" of tears and failure and despair. It is fascinating to watch. At the beginning of the process when my son was learning notes and rhythm, he experienced success and made the kind of progress we could see. It felt good and the momentum kept us going. And then, as he mastered that part of the mechanics, he began to learn the art of piano playing. This is a different thing. It is certainly not for the weak-minded, weak-tempered, or weak-stamina-ed. Here is where self-esteem is earned the hard way and progress cannot be seen from lesson to lesson. Instead, all of sudden after several months, we will both realize that something foreign is coming off the keys, something richer, more tempered, and more musical. And then we both have a rush of pure joy, knowing sometime, somewhere, it all came together and he stepped forward an inch.

But my story is not about the long haul. My story is about our Missoula teacher. In fact, he is an extraordinary pianist and teacher, but someone who I would call a purist. Piano-playing and teaching are tasks that he considers deeply intellectual and real only when the student aspires to reaching the highest heights of musicality. Things like popularity, external success, and public accolades are, to him, most likely the signs of sub-standard playing and cloying to the uninitiated. He plays for a higher standard and a deeper purpose, and his ability to remain true to his inner music amazes me. He also happens to be a co-conspirator of sorts from Saturday to Saturday. Trained in New York City and author of his own style of music, he has lived in Missoula for "only" about 35 years, as he says, and considers himself a passer-through here. He presents a different type of character than someone like Badwater Bill, who became authentic the moment his car turned west off the Maryland Turnpike.

Our Missoula teacher has lived here almost half of his life, but not the half that mattered, apparently. New York City is still ingrained in his bearing and being. When we met him he introduced himself as a talker who was out of place, caught now in a world of smoke signals and verbal parsimony. I laughed and laughed. Since then, we have become used to the unleashed torrent of Saturday words and come to enjoy the stories and sidebars that he provides as he and my son dance in front of the piano in the most contorted forms imaginable making music that aches and pains with its beauty. He is, although he does not see it, as authentic a Montanan as Badwater Bill, though. His is more a civilizing mission than a "join in and join up" one, but he stands guard at the frontiers of reason as molded and shaped by this land as any cattle rustler or herd drover ever was. Yesterday he told us that he had enjoyed teaching us (we are both students of some sort or another) and that some days he thought he would run away from here and go to Atlanta to find students like us. "But there are no students like us in Atlanta," I thought. Why, if this is who we really are at heart, we are not even ourselves in Atlanta! Not because we are hypocrites, although I suppose we are hypocrites, too, most days, but because it is the change of place and focus that has brought delight and present-living into our lives and that is what he senses in us. It made me think how powerfully positive it is for everyone when we dare to live authentically. It made me think that with all the human ingenuity in this world to make things like cheese-in-a-can, squeegee cloths that can soak up a small pond, and no-touch car washes, why can't someone come up with a way for us to bottle wide-eyed wonder, open hearts and minds, thrill at the start of each new day, and delight in encountering the unknown? Why can't we take a dose from time to time wherever we live, a double dose when life gets rough, and be ourselves all the time?

Our conversation made me smile, though, as I thought about the Shampoo Bar I had seen earlier on my way to his house. Juxtaposing those images of a virtuoso piano player trapped in a neighborhood not five blocks from the Shampoo Bar, I cringed to think that he would ever want to leave this place. After all, isn't it the constant rubbing and painful friction of the rock tumbler that shines the jewels? Isn't beauty more visible in a place where it can be seen because it is highlighted? He belongs here, in the spotlight of the "last best place," as Montanans say. Here is where his sheen deepens by the hour and his tough and pure vision of what piano playing and life should both be gets a chance to come to life. As humans, I guess we all get caught "looking over the fence," but maybe that is why we should listen to the people who wander through our pastures when they tell us, "It is good enough here. That is why we came through."

Today we stuck our first bumper sticker on the car that has carried us across this country. It says, "Get Lost," and in tiny letters underneath, "in Montana." We did that and it has been all good. The view from nowhere is the best one of all.

The Piano Lesson

Monday, February 25: (27°F, low, snow; 36°F, high)

Here in Montana they love their dogs. Some travel in pick-up cabs, some in long-beds, and others are in the family sedan jumping over seats back and front to bark. They ride to the post office, the Valley market, the school, sidekicks to their owners' daily lives. And you cannot always match the dog to the owner. One day I came out of the post office to a large, black truck pulling in beside me with a rumbling muffler, and leaning over his owner's lap was a medium-sized black poodle with a haircut in bobbles and puffs, looking in all his get-up like an upscale, fancy city dog. One evening we pulled into The Hungry Bear for pizza beside an open-bed truck with a dog kennel in back, but the dog loose. A beautiful border collie sat in the back of that truck beside his kennel with snow pouring all over him, patiently waiting for his owner to wrap up his night so that they could go home. My own dog barked like madness had descended upon her, but this collie sat and stared at her and then looked at The Hungry Bear restaurant-bar-casino door and seemed to sigh, "the grief I put up with...."

Most people we know have dogs, but these Montana dogs are not like the dogs I know. At my house in Georgia there are two types of dogs: one type runs in packs and sometimes also straggles through the neighborhoods singly cruising around house by house to follow some path only they see. Even our county park ranger lets her dogs run free in our public park, where they are a menace, and yet no one dares say anything for fear of being seen as rude. In fact, most days they lounge around under the "No Dogs Allowed Off Leash" sign posted at the entrance. And then the "responsible dog owners" all have fences and leashes and every type of toy and chew made, keeping their pets tied to them in every way possible and looking, for all intent and purposes, as if they have some kind of zoo in the back yard. Here our neighbors have dogs; in fact, yesterday Bubba almost walked into us, causing my dog to bark as if she had encountered a grizzly bear emerging early from hibernation. But Bubba's owner just said, "Knock it off, Bubba," and he slunk back home quickly, obedient to the T.

Even the *Confederados* have two dogs, and they come out, get their work business done, and go back inside, very obedient and over-fed and happy. The vet was right when she told me that people love their dogs here.

One thing, though, that all dog owners agree on is that dogs should not chase wildlife. By this they mean deer, really. I mean deer wander through the front yard, back yard, side yard, across the street, in the middle of the street, along both sides of the street. Utterly unperturbed, they glare at dogs and people much like I would a horde of mosquitoes – something to bear and put up with as a necessary environmental irritant. The troop that lives between our cabin and the neighbor's house is usually composed of nine animals and they move around a few yards here and there, but not too far. Every time I take Kalispell out for a walk, they trot in front of us to go over the hill, sometimes lifting their heads and peeking at us as we walk, and then two hours later they repeat it again, having returned to their grousing area sometime in the meantime. Kalispell stays on leash, because Georgia dogs are not well trained when faced with deer. In Georgia no self-respecting dog would let nine deer live in her yard. She walks forward pulling with all her might and making me thankful that I am a substantial creature of weight, and then stops abruptly so that I miss a step and create a little give in the leash. With this tiny give in the tautness, she takes a step backwards and then lunges fiercely, trying to pull me along. So I pull her back and tell her to settle down, while my neighbor huffs out a quick, "That's enough, Bubba," and Bubba obeys. But don't worry too much about Bubba's inability to express himself; when I go to the post office in the morning, Bubba will be the one that barks his head off at me from a front-end cab.

Tuesday, February 26: (24°F, low, light snow and windy; 38°F, high)

    Bernice's Bakery in Missoula is reason alone to travel from Georgia to Montana. It pitches itself as "Old World" with crusty and chewy breads all baked on site, but it is 100% Montana. Packed into an old warehouse building as old as Missoula, with un-yuppified brickwork and exposed ductwork, a loft-former-attic where old tables and bakery equipment are haphazardly (and perilously) stored right over the bakers' heads, and not more than ten small tables crammed together for the admiring public, it is the junction of the intellectual elite, avid sports enthusiasts, devoted dog owners, stressed college students, and discriminating food critics who all come together to savor and relish what is surely the best pastry I have ever eaten in my life. Without a doubt in my mind, Bernice's can take on any pastry shop anywhere and best them in the competition.

    I don't know what other people value at Bernice's, although everybody has their favorite, because everything – *and I mean everything* – is usually sold out long before lunch, but the spanakopita is by far our favorite. In fact, we high-tail it to Bernice's as early as possible on Saturdays so that we can get a slice of it because by 9:00 a.m. it is usually sold out. The bakery sits beside the Clark Fork River and, even during winter's coldest days, it is not unusual to see a whitewater fanatic out on the currents. It is also not unusual to see the fanatic park the kayak and climb up the bank to get pastry.

    And as if the pastries themselves are not sufficient bounty, Bernice's caters to all species. Beside the register there is a big glass container filled with homemade leftover pastry dog biscuits, so we always get our goodies and then two-to-go for our canine car mates barking and salivating down the windows as they wait for us impatiently. Even they recognize Bernice's. As soon as we park, they "get in position" at each door facing the shop and wait until we emerge with their goodies. And there are Saturdays when Bernice's runs out of what we want and we start looking at those dog biscuits as suitable emergency substitutes....

Do-it-yourself is more than an attitude in this city. It is also a flavor. In fact, all over Missoula there are "unique eats" where bakers, chefs, average Grandmas, and sometimes questionable Uncle Bobs pull out extraordinary fare that amazes us. In my own town in Georgia, virtually every restaurant is chain, the groceries are chain, and the expectation from the public is stunningly low (except for the Caramel Cake from the Bulloch House in Warm Springs, which is worth a drive back to Georgia). But in Missoula, things look different. You can strike out, you can put food out that misses the mark, you can come out with a combination that mystifies or even bamboozles but you absolutely, unconditionally, without a doubt, cannot be unoriginal or inauthentic. That is unforgiveable here. That will cost you the clientele. So on Saturdays at lunch, although Bernice's is certainly our highlight of the early part of the day, we take courageous forays into culinary mazes and experience things that we have – *so far* – lived to tell about another day. And most Saturdays, we experience true wonderment – delicious food, interesting décor, and enthusiastic servers and public who truly act as if they are sharing the best of themselves. Who knew that going out to eat could be the best communion ever?

Wednesday, February 27: (24°F, low, partly cloudy; 44°F, high)

I have never seen a school like the one my son attends. It is energetic, open, engaging, and fun. Tomorrow after-school Nordic skiing ends for the year, and soon after-school mountain biking will begin, but today they started another sports program to involve a different set of children and to involve the skiers as they transition out of their program for the season. They now have an After-School Fitness Club with jump rope, running, and various warm-up exercises. Today we passed the open door and heard Bach playing in the background and about 20-25 kids occupied at various "stations" doing work out. Sponsored by the school and manned by the gym teacher and volunteers, it looked very compelling and inviting with lots of kids and some teachers participating. We passed by longingly to go practice piano in the multi-purpose room with its all-in-one rock-climbing wall, theater staging area, ski storage area, and cafeteria in the back of the school. I also noticed today they have a big new salad bar in the space and a huge bulletin board entitled, "Healthy Eating on the Go," where the school chef posts pictures of children eating something healthy while practicing some type of sport activity (eating an apple on skis, carrot sticks while trekking, or a pack of peanuts while twirling on the ice skating pond!)

The beauty of all this is that there does not seem to be anything fake about it. The school is not promoting physical activity because they were told to do this or because of high obesity rates in this population (because there doesn't seem to be nearly as much here as in the South); for all intent and purposes, they are doing this because they like it and it is fun! The school chef did tell us that he is competing to win a $5,000 grant to buy new cafeteria tables for the children by having the "healthiest lunchroom in the state" and he worked outside on the snowed-over playing fields to groom a large cross-country skiing track where children can opt to ski for recess and after-school fun if they wish. But none of this is contrived in any sort of awkward way. It is as if the primary and most important message for the children is that as humans we are a sum total of muscles – from the brain to the body and all in between, it is about engaging, being present, and enjoying interactions with others.

We never leave the school before 4-4:30, because of our own piano practice, but I also never walk out of there without seeing that building with its gyms, (snow) fields, and classrooms still open and filled with active kids and parents and a handful of committed teachers. Some evenings, after dinner, we think about going back over there to play ball or chat with locals. It is a true community recreation center, where the word "recreation" literally means to bring anew. What a shining model for other schools to emulate. It reminds me of something that I have discovered in my own everyday space at home in Georgia. Cramped as we are in our 1140 square foot house with the piano not more than six feet from the kitchen stove, I often feel unexpected gratitude that our house is simple and small because my son's daily practice is also my cooking routine. We do both of these things together in a strange sort of way and share our lives more intensely and joyfully. When I was little, we had a music room in our house. Feeling banished there to practice, away from the center of activity, I grew to dislike my time at the piano. Having more meant enjoying it less.

I think it might be precisely because the school is the scene of community activity that it is so loved and cared for by everyone in the town. Used from sun-up to sun-down, it is a place where people want to volunteer and invest, to dream and to practice, to enjoy and applaud. A good model for all of us, everywhere.

The School Chef's Healthy Meals

Thursday, February 28: (26°F, low, morning snow; 42°F, high)

There were some things I expected when I came to Montana. For example, I expected winter roads in excellent condition, the best homemade soup in America, deer wandering in front of cars at will, trophy heads mounted inside any reputable restaurant, saloons and casinos peppered across the landscape on every corner, bad traffic in Missoula, speed limits that allow amateurs to practice NASCAR, friendly local townspeople, and the kind of scenes that make your heart ache, your jaw fall open, and your right foot press on the brake. But I never figured on a prohibition against left-hand turns. That one caught me off guard.

It seems that some Montanans, especially those in any type of urban area, are very much opposed to the left. You can go right, you can go roundabout, you can go up or down, but you may not under any circumstances during the light of day, go left in downtown Missoula. Traveling down South Higgins from Brooks, I imagine one-way Third St. and Bernice's Bakery on the corner and have a deep desire for an English scone (because after 9:00 a.m. you must stop the unreasonable desire for spanakopita). I slow down, put on my blinker, come to a stop one block ahead on Fourth, and then notice a sign suspended from the street cable that reads, "NO LEFT TURNS." "What a bother!" I think, and so I cross the bridge over the Clark Fork River, circle around down East Main, back onto Orange, go back southward, cross the Clark Fork again, now in the opposite direction, and return to Higgins via Brooks, thinking I will make my left turn earlier and then head to Bernice's a back way, but, alas, even on Fifth St., which permits a one-way movement leftward in theory because it is a one-way street going in that direction, there is a sign suspended above that reads, "NO LEFT TURNS." Amazing! You can travel left in Missoula, but it is very difficult to *turn left*. This is a brilliant way to prevent downtown traffic. So I did the Big Circle again, but this time I knew to turn left on Third St. off of Orange and head northward on that one-way to Bernice's and avoid Higgins at all costs.

Kalispell? Same thing. We rode into town at high noon, after spending big bucks at Murdoch's Ranch store on things like saddle blankets, ropes, and horseshoes to be repurposed in Georgia for rugs and wall art, and traveled eastward on Main.

First, we had to do a tight roundabout to bypass the courthouse with its sign, "PRISONERS MUST BE HANDCUFFED FROM BEHIND," and then we headed on into town, passing Montana Wheat on our right. We saw a lovely shop on the left side, absolutely no traffic, and some parking right off the street. I slowed down, put on my blinker for kicks, and stopped, careful not to break any rules in a town that takes all of its visitors through a roundabout with a sign that reads "PRISONERS MUST BE HANDCUFFED FROM BEHIND" and then saw it. It was suspended on the street cable just like in Missoula and read "NO LEFT TURNS." I admit I was a sallow creature and I gave up. I went down to the next corner, made a right, went another block, made a right, again another block, another right, and then faced the redlight on Main again. There, at last, on a signal, I could make a left and go westward again and head back to the Valley, where right and left have no meaning because the lakes are all on one side and geographically prohibit left-hand turns everywhere. Either the same person worked for city planning in both Missoula and Kalispell or they were classmates in Montana City Planning 101 and both made As. In any event, it takes ingenuity, courage, and a Wild West "can-do" attitude to drive in Montana cities.

MARCH

Friday, March 1: (34°F, low, very foggy and dripping; 48°F, high)

It amazes me to consider how much beauty aches. This morning our world became more beautiful, a concept that continues to defy my own understanding. How can beauty become intensified if it is already beautiful? But the weather shifts more perceptibly now. This morning it was 34 degrees at 4:30 a.m. and I could hear the drips of melting snow and ice pelting the roof in ¾ time… "plop, plop, plop-plop…." As the sky lightened, I began to see strange shapes and shadows, so I leashed up my dog and we went for a walk in the increasingly slushy and slippery snow. As the break-up starts, the depth of our trail increases – once walking firmly on snow bridges and packed accumulation, we are now traversing pits and fallen branches and little streams where the snow underworld has begun to wake up. It is disconcerting to be walking on a "known path" and feel my footing slide into an invisible rut. It is both disconcerting and delightful to wake up and discover my world is being re-made. We walked along the logging road and ran into three of our deer friends. This morning, instead of walking away from us at a leisurely pace, they slowly walked around us and up the hill and stepped right over the top and challengingly peeked at us. Antler-less at this time of year, they were all ears and a low sloped forehead with two small-ish eyes. If I spoke to them, they ducked their heads back, but when I looked silently, they watched me back. Even my dog stared, unsure if these were the real things or some new type of yard ornament gracing the hilltop.

Our walk this morning was compelling. Because of the warm-up and shifting axis, our world has become magically filtered with fog and dripping - silence and shadow filling pockets here and there. At times, as I walked Kalispell, we entered a foggy pocket and were alone in the world, and then we re-emerged, peeked back at the deer patiently waiting for our return, and knew we had "promises to keep" as this day advanced. We turned back toward the cabin.

Melting Snow

Montana Winter Days

Saturday, March 2: (28°F, low, mostly clear; 51°F, high)

Our dogs have discovered a new way of hunting now that we are in the Big Sky Country. Leashed up when walking around outside, unable to do anything about the wildlife that walks around, in front of, behind, and beside them everywhere we go, and that appears to be mocking them and sometimes us, they are like baited bulls in the car. Free at last, they attack deer, elk, and even bald eagles with impunity from both the back and front seats, hurling themselves from one end to the other, right over our heads, when they spot their prey. Helpless, we duck or hang onto the wheel while they relentlessly pursue their targets. Sometimes frustrated and half-deafed, I pull over and try to get them to settle down, but as long as the wild animals remain, our dogs continue devoted to the hunt. Dogs normally thrilled about the leash and a long walk, now pull us toward the car when we take them out and beg us to let them ride on a hunt, even if it is only to the post office. After all, the chances of encountering wildlife here from the comfort of your car, is very near 100 percent.

Sunday, March 3: (34°F, low, very windy, small blizzard in a.m.; 33°F, high)

From one minute to the next, Old Man Winter shook his fist ferociously at us this morning, demanding respect we were beginning to dismiss. We got lulled yesterday by the heavy melting and rushing rivulets of snow and ice transformed into mere water into thinking that Winter was leaving us. But this morning it re-asserted itself as if to say that the earth may turn as it will, but Winter will not go until it is good and ready! I took the garbage out at 6:45 a.m. and by 7:00 there was a rather terrific wind. At first I thought it was blustery and squally, but then it became very angry and grim for about 30 minutes. Snow was whipped this way and that, heavy falling and blizzard-like. The deer in the front yard began prancing as if they were members on a relay team waiting for Santa's sleigh. And the cats glued themselves to the front window, drawn by the howling wind and pelting snow.

An ingénue in this world, I grabbed my dog and thought it would be glorious to step into the winter swell. She, more prudent than I, pulled back at first and looked around inquisitively, momentarily unsure, and then gave in to her Russian steppe heritage and bolted, dragging me with her. We lunged towards the logging road and its hill turning white literally before our eyes. The deer that had now moved to the side of our cabin ran down the hill in our front yard to get away from us and the dog arched up trying to spring after them, ready for the chase in this new world gone awry. It took all my might to reel her back in and back onto the road. Trudging along in my long flannel nightgown, snow boots with no socks and no scarf for my ears, wind plummeting temperatures and my legs permanently exposed as the nightgown whipped this way and that and sometimes up over my chest, I can only say that we must have looked like fools to the wind and snow and trees. Even more foolish still when I turned her around and started back, only to discover that going westward on the road was really going into the wind. I had to pull up my collar to cover my nose so that I could breathe and my ears started screaming with the wind and snow. The dog, somewhat cowed at last, pushed her head downward and moved into the snow like a pack mule. We didn't have too far to get back, but it was further than I would have thought. And then, about 20 minutes after we returned, it stopped. The snow became fine and tamed and the wind deserted us. It was just a reminder, "Kilroy is here" somewhere, watching.

The Kilroy Wind

Monday, March 4: (19°F low, partly cloudy; 33°F, high)

Last week we went to practice piano in the multi-purpose room after school. It's a routine that we frequently follow, although sometimes we detour and go to the small church and practice on their piano, especially on weekends or when the multi-purpose room gets too loud. The church's doors are always unlocked and they welcome us to come in whenever we want. But the benefits of the school are unexchangeable – there, I can fuss at my son and count the rhythm out loudly and exasperatedly and he can practice his "dark" Schumanns and the boogie woogie of the New York train song without feeling that we are defiling the space.

So anyhow, last week we went into the school practice area and found a jolly man perched in front of the Kimball, tuning away. He was sitting on top of a large drum wedged between the Wurlitzer pushed perpendicularly to it and a large handmade glider leaning on the other side of the piano. There was no bench in sight. And all over the area there were drums and boxes and deconstructed (very large) xylophone keys scattered on the floor like the remains of a barroom brawl. Only a very agile person could even get to the Kimball, much less tune it, I thought. The Steinway that we use is pulled out and sits haphazardly in the middle of the room against a shelving unit used as a divider. Its key cover is broken and we have had to wedge a book into the face of the piano to get the top to stay put. At first we salvaged it out of the morass of things on a daily basis and hunted for the bench, but now after more than six weeks of this, people have left the Steinway sitting there in the middle of the floor and re-purposed it as a desk and table. Most days now we only have to remove used food items, ski boots, books, and xylophone parts.

We hollered at the piano tuner from across the room, unable to get near him, and he bellowed back, "Hello! Are you the piano player, young man?" We introduced ourselves and he came scrambling over the debris field and greeted us heartily, saying he was an itinerant piano tuner from Bozeman. Delighted and amazed at his athletic ability, I thanked him for coming and told him how much this would help my son and that I appreciated how welcoming the school had been about my son's piano practice. "Well," he said, "there's a story behind this. You see, I came today to the church to tune their piano, and the pastor there told me that there was a little boy from Georgia who was very good on piano and who sometimes practiced here in the school, but that his mother said the piano was out of tune here. So, I finished at the church and came by here and told them they needed their piano serviced as well, now that it was being played. And the superintendent told me to go ahead and tune one of them and that this Kimball was the one in best shape." "Oh," I responded, "we don't use that Kimball because we can't get over there to it. We use the Steinway." "Well," he said, "let me hear your son play," leaving me to think he was requesting an audition to see if he should petition the superintendent to let him tune more than one of the three assorted pianos there. So my son played on the Steinway and he came up (I should have watched how he extricated himself this time from the Kimball area so that I could re-trace his steps) and he patted him on the back and said, "That's really cool! You need all these pianos tuned with a talent like that! Next time I come through I'll tell the superintendent and plan to stay here a while to get them all in shape."

We practiced and then started out of the school past the main office. The superintendent, a young and very pleasant man, was standing there with some papers in his hands talking to the coach. I interjected gratitude for the tuning and he said, "Well, I thought what he said was right. As long as you all are here, we might as well tune the best of the three pianos. In fact, I was thinking we might just clean up that room sometime, too." I didn't tell him that we couldn't actually physically get to the Kimball, but I did see a note on the piano the next day that the tuner had left there. My son crawled under the debris and around the Wurlitzer and read it. It said, *"This piano will not hold the tuning more than a few days. It will take more than one tuning to get it settled."* So, alas, I guess the Steinway will still be the best deal of the three within a day or two despite good intentions. It has the added advantage that we can actually get to it.

The Ebullient Piano Tuner

Tuesday, March 5: (7°F, low, sunny; 48°F, high)

I admit that I have lived a very "suburban" life, sometimes on the fringes of the accelerated pace of a large metropolis like Atlanta and occasional long-term visitor to more exotic places like Lima, Peru, and Buenos Aires, Argentina, but most frequently I have lived in smaller urban areas such as Greenville, SC, Madison, WI, or semi-rural towns like Carrollton, GA, where farming and cattle-raising continue to be big business. In fact, one of my favorite activities at home is to go to the Sale Barn and hear the auctions of livestock that still begin at high noon every Monday. One semester I even took my university class over to the Barn so that they would learn about their own heritage and learn to appreciate it.

But, overall, I am not very exposed to auctions, haggling, and wheeling and dealing. And, gambling is not legal in Georgia which, by the way, does not mean that it does not occur; it just means that it is unregulated and not out in the visible sphere of public life and that people like me don't have experience gambling. Here, gambling in its various forms is quite common. In fact, I have never bought gas in Montana where there was not also a casino running in front, back, on top of, below, or by the side of the pumps. They are ubiquitous. But as far as I can see, there is no increased delinquency, poverty, or damnation in Montana over other states. These places become a simple part of the landscape as we move across it.

As we first contemplated traveling out West during the school year, I did some research and talked with my son's principal and we discovered that Montana and Georgia were "mostly" both on the new Common Core standards for public education; mostly, as it happens, Georgia has not yet gone all the way in Social Studies and Science. But in sum and substance, we figured the exchange of one quarter of academics between there and here would be overall, relatively, harmless. With great enthusiasm, his teachers packed a large folder filled with all kinds of "Georgia Standards" work in the two unconverted subject areas, all saddled with a "can-do" attitude that this trip would benefit far more than harm, and we headed off into the sunset.

But education is much, much more than standards. Education is not a science where you can prescribe and write down and enforce exactly every move a teacher should make.

Education is an art. I think if we were to embrace this, strengthen humanities in our schools and universities, then the clarity and precision of science and math would both have better ballast and would be more successful than our current miserable status. For a dyed-in-the-wool scientist, the relativity of the humanities is as gut-wrenching as entering the ninth level of purgatory and for many advanced cultural anthropologists, the precision of math is very alluring after a day of arguing in the trenches for the smallest of gains. What a relief to yell out the answer and hear someone say, "Correct!" As I tell my anthropology students regarding rods and cones in the miraculous human eye, sometimes when we look directly at something in the dark, it mostly disappears, because night vision comes from the side rods and not the sophisticated cones in the middle. As someone else once said somewhere, "Sometimes the most direct path is the one that takes a detour or two on the way." It's kind of like that in education, I think. The precise accuracy of writing and ciphering pales in importance to the marked imprecision of things like excitement, inspiration, drive, creativity, curiosity, and ingenuity. Science and math plumb these areas for their greatest success and when these areas are lacking, the beauty of science is eclipsed by the rote formulaic way of doing things the only way we know how. That isn't science – it is just technical application. One new unforeseen challenge and it all goes dark again.

  Well, really that is neither here nor there for this story, because my point is that my son has learned both Common and Uncommon Core while here. Because the school is small, there are just at 100 students in a Pre-K to 8th grade institution, and the principal also happens to be the superintendent reigning over a district of one, things get done efficiently and in the moment when inspiration occurs. No need to file loads of paperwork to make requests for the smallest of things, like a walk outside on a pretty day; just run down the hall and tell the secretary where she can find you if some parent needs to contact their child while you are out of the classroom. You need a bus to take your class skiing? Run down the hall while they are getting their skis on. You want to use the school for community chorus? Run by the school and tell them. In fact, this informality extends even further: one day we went to practice piano after school and found the community handbell choir in our normal space, except they had pushed aside the piano and stacked all the chairs and flipped the bench up on top of some shelves to get it out of the way. The director, who knew we practiced there on Tuesdays, smiled at us and shook her keys telling us to take these and walk up the road to her house where we were welcome to practice on her piano. "My house isn't big enough for the choir, but it's just right for you two." I was stunned. We barely knew each other by sight and I had never been to her house. Wow. Her offer was a testimony to community.

So all this is to say that my son's classroom is as much a part of the mentality here as anything else and I am always delightfully surprised to hear about the next thing they are doing in there. Following Common Core in its spirit and not the letter of the law, my son's very experienced teacher delights at making his class his own. When they studied weights and measures in science, he had them design and build bridges with saws and knives, balsa wood, and glue. In fact, they had a veritable workshop going on every afternoon at the end of the day. And when it came to math, he devised practice in a skill that had as much practical application in Montana as learning to hunt squirrels does in Georgia: the auction. Now at my son's school in Georgia, they can earn points and school money by good behavior and go on a shopping spree during the semester to buy pencils and stickers and other rather useless items. But here, in a town with only three small stores and a gas station, that is not a very useful skill. So here my son has learned how to auction. During the week he hawks out items we have brought from Georgia or purchased here and takes them to school to be auctioned on Friday.

The 5th grade Auction works just like a real one, helping students hone a useful local skill, although some of the prices are worthy of a hearty laugh. On the first Friday my son participated (his teacher "gave" him $600 to start with), they had up for bid a set of tokens for the carousel in Missoula. The bidding war got fierce between my son and another boy, a real Wild West shoot-out, and my son paid $600 for ten tokens worth $7.50 otherwise. Having bankrupted the Easterner, the class went on to purchase wood coasters, dishes, and trinkets the children had lifted from their homes on their way to school. My son came home proud of his purchase and began hunting and gathering around the rented cabin and in our suitcases for auction items so that he could "build up my auction purse" again. Today I sent him to school with an iron elephant I reluctantly purchased as part of a set with a horse I wanted. He was thrilled to get back in on the "money pool." On Fridays we wait expectantly to see what the haul will be for the day. Talk about getting the whole family involved with education....they know how to do that here. (Postscript for 3/8/14: my son purchased a small ski cap for $900 this week. What a bargain!)

Wednesday, March 6: (23°F, low, rain/snow/sun; 44°F, high)
We must have hit that magic time when we have been thoroughly vetted and are now, for better or worse, worth

getting to know. The scientific proof of it is in the fact that in five days three different people, wholly and totally unconnected, have done the same thing; they have asked us who we are and why we came. Apparently the possibility that we came for snowmobiling, especially as the weather shifts to spring in surreptitious ways, no longer holds water and so the question must be asked, "Who are you people and why have you not left yet?"

It first happened at a craft store in town where a person who we see at church and in the store suddenly connected the two scenes and warmly greeted us to find out more about why we were staying here so long. Friendly, helpful, and seemingly relieved to now have us better figured out, she became an instant friend after seven weeks. Then the next morning we went to the gas station for Wi-Fi and coffee and the sales clerk starting quizzing us about where we were actually living in town and then triumphantly announced, "You are my neighbors!" We experienced as much glee as she because we love our neighbors, even though we don't know their names. No kidding. During the winter storms and days of trudging up the driveway and wondering if we would ever get the car back up our hill, it was reassuring and bonding to wave at people across the snowbank and listen to their dogs, their snowmobile engines, and their wood chopping. Even though we had not formally met, I always imagined that we could go there if we needed help. And now there was a very friendly smile and welcome to tie us in place at the cabin. We chatted like old friends, so accustomed to each other's routines and lifestyles even though we had never met before.

And then three days later, it happened again. We were eating at a local diner, as we normally do on Tuesdays, and the waitress, who we had seen several times, asked me if I was working at the local school because she had seen me there for several weeks. Like the other two conversations, our interaction was warm and welcoming, humble and hearty. How easy it would be to live here, I think. We have already passed through the "breaking in" time. We went through the watching time, testing time, probing time, and now we are worthwhile and here only a short time longer. It really breaks my heart. All three of these people would be such delightful friends – all three quickly began to tell their own stories to make me laugh. And I saw again what I have seen all along...people struggling, working hard, suffering the normal issues of all of our lives, but people who feel as if they are living in the midst of something special. All three women, one extremely talkative, one more reticent and serious, and the other young and a bit unsure of herself, quickly laughed about their lives and asserted their own can-do attitude, telling their troubles and then making a proclamation that it was all still worth it and they would "carry on." Our conversation could only be described as a joyful commiseration. We all had problems, we all were rubbing nickels together in one way or another, but at least they lived here – in paradise.

Thursday, March 7: (23°F, low, partly cloudy; 42°F, high)

Now it is all beginning to come together: the people in our town are committed to physical exercise and promoting a healthy lifestyle in the schools not because First Lady Michelle Obama set the standard, but because there is no help to be had if you get sick. Talk about dismantling the health care system – here it has imploded from within in the strangest way I've ever heard. Sometime about a week and a half ago, the small appointment-only medical clinic here had its own small emergency when the water heater broke and leaked from upstairs to downstairs and out the door, leaving behind an in-house ice skating rink. Tragic, indeed, and something too many of us can identify with. In fact, even while I've been here on my sojourn, my neighbor reported that my own water heater had broken and flooded my garage in Georgia. Alas, this is an understandable mess and I was very sympathetic at first.

That was the first week after the incident. Then I got all confused again. Last week the local newspaper reported that the clinic will be "closed indefinitely for repairs." Huh? The only professional medical attention in an almost 60-mile radius + water damage from a water heater = indefinite closure. Now I'm sure I'm missing some facts, but in this town where the mass of people build their own homes, house construction materials are plentiful, no one has the business they need to get through the winter and everyone is looking for clients, and sickness has been some of the highest reported in this area in years (this was the warning they whispered to us in Missoula about influenza through the Valley), there is no way to reinstate medical attention in the town, apparently. In addition, when we went to the clinic to see if they could attend my son for an upper respiratory infection about a month ago, they told us they were much too busy and we would be seen more quickly if we went to Missoula. So it certainly seems reasonable that a medical clinic is needed and reinstatement of medical attention should be at least a moderate priority. But, alas, I got that one wrong. After two weeks, the clinic remains closed, no provisions are given for anyone who might need them, and life goes on.

Last night I asked someone about this. I said that this was apparently a busy place and I could not understand how they could just close up "indefinitely." The local told me, "Well, the one time I needed them because I had a concussion, they told me they couldn't handle that and I would have to go to

Missoula, concussion and all." Hmm…this one has stumped me.

The (Former) Health Clinic

Friday, March 8: (17°F, low, sunny; 45°F, high)

Every day after school my son and I go back into the multi-purpose room so that he can practice piano (some days we go to the church, but mainly it is the school). And as I pass through the halls, I keep a running account of all the things going on in the classrooms from their bulletin boards. There are some great things happening – one class has made space helmets out of paper plates and has each child's face like an astronaut's posted on the hall board. It is very humorous and creative. Another class has a board of "Class Book Recommendations" as if they were a Barnes & Noble. Each child reads a level book and then draws a picture and answers a series of questions: "What I Liked," "What I Didn't Like," "Summary" and "I Would/Would Not Recommend This Because...." Some of the things they write are really funny. You can tell life's critics by the earliest of ages and after reading all of the write-ups, it is evident that the book either fed or didn't a position that the child already held toward reading and certain topics long before the book landed in their hands.

But, anyhow, this week I saw the large bulletin board beside the library door filled with a beautiful map of the Iditarod in Alaska. It was labeled IDITAREAD, and the route from Anchorage to Nome was marked by a very colorful line showing lots of historic detail, including the "Odd Years" route and the "Even Years" route and the places along the journey. It was also well-marked with mileage posts. And there were four little colorful handmade flags placed along the route. One flag in bold letters said "DOGS" and the others said "4th," "5th," and "6th" and beside the big laminated map there was a clipboard which listed the points that each class had earned each day so far, converted into a Mileage Log. I stopped my son and we discussed the board. He was very excited about it. You see, every day they check the news and find out where the dogs have actually reached and mark it on their map (the dogs stay dreadfully ahead of the children, by the way) and then each teacher tallies up the points that each child in that grade earns on reading for the day (the children earn accelerated reading points – called AR points - on every book based on its level of difficulty and how well they answer the questions on the computer-generated test) and then converts the points into miles and moves their token flag along the route to compete with the other grades. I thought this was incredibly creative! Current events, local culture (because here they also have dog sled races and most of them know people participating in the Iditarod every year), energetic competition, mathematics and reading – it was all there, together. The pride of living here – as opposed to there, wherever there is – starts in grade school.

Saturday, March 9: (20°F, low, sunny; 52°F, high)

I am my own worst demon. I suspect some of this is the human condition, but some of it is my own personal weakness. I worry, I plan, I attempt to control, and I work ahead of the assignment at hand. As soon as March commenced, this condition started. Time, marked by humans into increments of seconds, minutes, hours, days, weeks, months, and years allows us to calibrate passage and movement as if they were material things. And so, people like me, start forecasting, predicting, and anticipating something that is not real and is not here. Once March commenced, I began a mindset that has been destructive – "this is our last month," I thought, and so a doleful countdown started in my mind. Today I thought, "Now we only have three weeks left here." I could say that I have fought this and am living "in the present" and for "now," but I am only moderately successful at controlling these thoughts. I hear preachers, crooners, and old-timers tell me to live wisely and live for today – "let tomorrow take care of itself." And I experience some frustration with these invectives because although they are true in essence, they are impossible in practice for anyone who must take any sort of leadership in life – including parents, teachers, and generally responsible people. It is a question, instead, of moderation of thought – not eradication. To eradicate planning of all kinds would mean that we cease investing in our lives and those of others. So the challenge, the way I see it, is to live in the present while staying cognizant and responsible for the future as well.

So I have set the following challenge to myself. These are the last days, indeed, but they are also the transition time when I should replace some of my mournful sadness with anticipation of my homecoming. And so I sat outside today in the chill and thought about my little lean-to back porch in Georgia with the rickety white, metal table, and the wicker chair, a place where writing is warm and thoughtful for me. And I thought about my students, waiting somewhat impatiently as they send e-mails to try to secure a spot in my upcoming class on the American West. I remember what pulls me homeward instead of what loosens me from this Valley and these people. And I remember that there and here is really the same place – I leave this time, though, from here, with a broader and more capable toolkit for my life there, as I have learned more about people and myself.

I cannot stop thinking about the upcoming transition of place, but I can remember that while I work hard to stay here in my heart and mind these "last days," I also change the way I look towards the future and re-script the plan to include a person who has experienced such joy over the last few weeks.

Surely this makes me less capable of accurately forecasting, but more confident that "some of this will go back there with me."

The Writing Place

Sunday, March 10: (19°F, low, drizzle; 46°F, high)

Little by little the world is extricating itself from the vice of cold and ice and hard-packed snow and we are discovering things about our world that we did not know. In fact, we are living over top of a whole other layer of life. This morning I took the dog for a walk in the invigorating chill, but the warmth yesterday had prompted a lot of melting and uncovered a layer underneath that we did not know about – it's kind of like seasonal archaeology. This morning I saw that there are logs that mark out a backyard for the cabin, when I had thought that the driveway was seamless with the logging road behind us. This morning I had to lift my foot or I would have stubbed it against the emerging logs. And then all along the logging road was a collector's dream world of artifacts: a spool of black thread thrown up onto the hill, apparently by a reluctant seamstress; an empty pop tart sleeve from the pre-snow era now encrusted with dirt, small pebbles, and shaped into the ice like a shining diamond horseshoe; a plastic bag of pine cones whose use I am pondering; a large basketball hoop that cuts up quite dangerously and on which I have been treading for many weeks now (I wonder if they will raise it up and play basketball back on the logging road in the spring and summer?); an ice-encrusted penny that shines like a pot of copper in the sun; and an occasional used tissue that very well might have provenience from me or my household, as we have used this road far more than anyone else this winter. And then there are cans as well – various kinds of beers and sodas and soup and tinned meats. I picked up two that were loosed today – a Shasta cola and some kind of mango nectar. And there is a creel thrown out there as well – a reminder that this place can be a fisherman's friend or foe. I imagine some tourist outfitted to the gills with every kind of brand new fly fishing accoutrement and then finding out that this pursuit is definitely not for the uncoordinated, impatient, or unimaginative. It is a treasure hunter's dream, indeed, especially if the person is a recycler. And I am beginning to see some black mounds emerging like shell middens filled with likely treasures. The Jolly Rancher wrappers I have been retrieving are not the same. Clearly an area-appropriate candy, those wrappers are laying right on the surface, so I bet the deer could point out one of the polluters in a line up.

Oh, today in church the pastor said that the change of season was both a prayer and a praise. We discuss outdoor sports a lot in church. "Well, with these warm days snowmobiling will be behind us soon. But not to worry – dirt bike season is next." Another parishioner hollered out, "There is no end to fun here." The town was mostly all attending a memorial service today for a former coach and principal from the area who was much loved. The services are usually held in the high school gymnasium for well-known community members. We did not attend, as we did not know him, but we sensed the quiet mood of today throughout the community.

Dirt Bike Dreams

Monday, March 11: (33°F, low, snow and then sun – very windy; 47°F, high)

Sometimes it is good to be from "some other place." And sojourners can make us dream. Yesterday being from Georgia made me, at last, a local. After all, who you are is relative to where you find yourself. In front of my class I am "Dr. Snipes"; in front of my mother, I am a rather incompetent child at times; and in front of my son I am "Mama," that beguiling figure who instructs, disciplines, fails, succeeds, comforts, and loves. But yesterday all three of us and the fifty-some people in the gymnasium were simply "Americans," quirky and lovingly gullible to joy. It was exhilarating to be on a level playing field for a while.

Yesterday afternoon we traveled up in the Valley to hear a touring Celtic duo called "Men of Worth." One is from Ireland and lives in Oregon now and the other is Scottish and lives in Sacramento. Despite their current addresses, though, they are very much men of their respective countries. About 50 people attended in all and the event was like having a personal concert at your own home. They took requests, regaled us with melodious ballads and unrivaled skill in playing guitar, mandolin, bodhran, and mandolincello, and entered into conversation with us as we swung our legs and tapped our feet, sang along at familiar choruses, and laughed uproariously at their stories and each other. During intermission, I and some three others spoke with them about the music, and its informality and melancholic joy. They talked about the feel of agent-less bookings and management-free interactions, and we talked of how little of that is left in the music world today. As we finished intermission, though, I decided to join those making song requests, and I asked if they would play "And the Band Played Waltzing Matilda...." One of them asked me if I knew that this was an Australian song. I teasingly looked at him, smiled, and said, "If you'll play if for me, then it will be our song." Later, the room was stilled and quiet as we all listened to the lines of that haunting ballad, feeling our fragile sense of humanity and our strength in unity and togetherness.

How odd...I came northward in the Valley yesterday to a small little community of no more than 400 people and met people from other countries and other places. And it all felt just right. For a moment we all recognized the sojourns of our lives and how that one experience makes us all human, all alike, all in unison for song and conversation and for feeling the beautiful weight of it all.

Tuesday, March 12: (22°F, low, snow and mixed rain; 35°F, high)

I've been troubling about my awareness of leaving. It seems to have dimmed and diminished everything suddenly. I find myself looking at a piece of scenery or listening to a friend share a story while tears fill my eyes and my mind keeps reminding me... "this may be the last time." So this afternoon I took a walk and I thought a long time about this dilemma of sensing ends long before they are here. This is not the first time I have lived with this burdensome way of thinking. Once as my cat aged beyond 15 years, I worried endlessly about the future and allowed myself to lose our contentment together as I would hold her and cry for no reason except anticipation. I anticipated her death long before it came. This went on for three years. But life and death are of much more serious stuff than leaving behind Montana, so I thought a long time and tried to re-position my thinking.

I thought about our most wonderful travels before Montana when I did not have so much time available. Some of the longer trips lasted a week and the smallest "long trips" lasted two nights – I love two-night trips so much because you can get there, get settled, and then wake up to a whole full day somewhere! And then I thought about Montana and how we had three more weeks. Why that is significantly longer than our longest normal trips! I was thinking that I would try to wake up tomorrow thinking that we just got here and now I have a whole three weeks stretching out in front of me. It really is all about perspective. After thinking about this, I felt better. Yes, we still have a long, long time here. Enough time to smile hard, laugh deep, travel far, and meet great characters.

Wednesday, March 13: (34°F, low, light rain and then sun; 49°F, high)

We went to the garbage dump this morning and it dawned on me again how much the recycling center reflects local color and culture everywhere. I think someone heartier and with a more discerning proboscis should do a cultural study of garbage dumps. Everywhere they are distinct and exhibit certain characteristics of the area in question. This one is surely no exception.

At home our garbage dumps are called "Recycling Centers," which means that we have about eight medium-sized square dumpsters for mixed and kitchen garbage and six large rectangular ones for recycling newspaper, plastics, aluminum, glass, furniture, and hard metals. People bring absolutely everything to the dump there – sometimes we find bicycles, basketball hoops, porch railings, car parts, sofas, and Christmas trees, both wooden and plastic. If you think what you are dumping is "good," then you can lean it up against the Salvation Army box for clothes that is also located there along with a sign that says, "Swap Area." It's really a free-of-charge Secondhand Store. I kind of like the arrangement because we all drive into the "Center," which is actually a large graveled area with a chain-link fence around it and operate as if it were totally self-service to give and take. The "Center" is open seven days a week and twelve hours a day, always eager for garbage. One day I was pulling out a large chair that my cat had made into pulled pork and a client, an older man, drove up behind me and asked if I needed help. I said, "No," politely, but he understood that it meant "Yes," and so he helped me get it out of the back of my hatchback and then said, "Why this is a fine chair; it just needs some new upholstery on the arm rests." I agreed. And so he asked if he could put it in the back of his truck. "Sure," I said, actually glad that someone saw its value. I sure did, which is why I had it for 12 years in such poor condition. He left happy as a clam, either to fix the chair for himself or to fix it and sell it to another old man. Either way, good for him. There is an attendant that works at the Recycling Center, but he stays inside the heated and air-conditioned hut watching TV almost all the time. It is rare that we see him, and when we do, he just smiles and waves at us. His only job, apparently, is to open and close the fence, which he does right punctually, I must say.

    Here in western Montana, though, garbage "recycling centers" are not the same. Or perhaps they are the same thing except they are hyped up on steroids in a visceral sort of way. In any event, just like restaurant-casino-saloons, these are a different sort of beast here. And garbage is not a laughing matter. It is serious stuff. That is evidenced in various ways: the garbage dump is located about seven miles from town and up on the side flank of a large hill, and getting there requires driving on the main road and then off onto a sometimes very rutted dirt road, in moderate condition at best, with ice and snow in winter and mud, all mud, in spring; the garbage dump is open only three days a week and has attenuated hours on those days (10-4); the dump itself is surrounded by two fences – there is a large metal bar arm that is at the first entrance and then the chain-link fence that surrounds the actual site itself with the dumpsters is significantly higher than our Georgia fences and electrified. (I am not sure if the intent is to keep something in or keep something out.) At the electrification entrance a huge sign says S-T-O-P, and the attendants (sometimes as many as three people) come out to check your GHT (garbage hang tag) and to ask you if you are recycling and what you have; the attendants, dressed in orange reflector vests and fatigues, tell you where to put the recyclables, as if it is a constantly shifting situation that requires a guide, and then they point out which dumpster (of the five or six there) is open so that they fill each consecutively. Now in Georgia we leave all eight open and people fill them haphazardly at will; I can't imagine what someone from Carroll County would say if the attendant man left his hut at all, much less to tell them to dump into one specific dumpster. I think we would all get a laugh out of that. Here, I get nervous on garbage days and try to not go more than twice a month. I always am fearful that I am going to do something wrong there. It is like going into a military landfill and it is intimidating. One day I carried a medium-sized bit of cardboard and saw that there was nowhere to put it in the recycling bins and so started to put it into the mixed dumpster. It was like there was some kind of silent alarm that went off because two people came running towards me and told me brusquely to take it to the end of the row where there was a growing pile of corrugated cardboard that I just happened to see at the time they emerged from their Quonset hut.

Now don't get me wrong. The people working there are kind, but they are so serious that it makes me feel guilty that I have garbage at all. Garbage is a terrible thing, I admit, and I try to create as little as possible, but I do miss the relaxed carefree, "mill-about-and-find-a-treasure" attitude normal at my home. By the way, here the recycling center/garbage dump is called a Transfer Site. It is all business. That may explain why the fence is so high and electrified – it keeps out animals and any people not worthy to handle toxic waste.

The Garbage Dump

Thursday, March 14: (31°F, low, partly cloudy; 59°F, high)

Spring is definitively arriving and every day something else proclaims the shift in allegiance from all that is cold and quiet and crystalline to something tender, new, and yet ebullient and joyful in frivolous ways. The signs are all over reminding us that the shift in seasons is a world-changing event...over and over and over again.

It has become clear to us that this new season brings a total shift not only in temperature, but in colors, textures, sounds, smells, and inhabitants of every variety. New plants, new animals, new people, it is as if we had been playing on an Etchosketch and now someone slowly, but insistently, begins to shake us back and forth to wipe off the scene in which we had placed ourselves. Before our eyes, everything is changing increasingly quickly.

In one week's time we have encountered a literal abundance of new land. For two months we had no idea what our driveway was made of. This week we discovered small pebbles and dirt underneath, as small rivulets began cutting out a chasm in the packed snow and ice that once constituted our small driving hill. The water runs more rapidly every day, as the sun transforms a solid into a liquid and mud. Now I straddle an ice mound as a try to keep the car tires in the "solid ground" mud grooves when on the steep driveway. The frozen lake that I have gazed upon with bits of nostalgia and melancholia for two months is now pocked with thin ice forecasting a coming break-up. The color has changed from an opaque white to a translucent darkness revealing deep waters. The ice fishermen are nowhere to be seen. Our most immediate neighbors are getting closer to us, as our land starts merging into a hillside. All winter we have been separated by a large debris field of scraped snow and ice from two separate driveways, but little by little, we are conjoining so that you could use either driveway and get to either house. Yesterday I was even jolted by the sight of the Confederate flag rippling in the breeze of a cracked window. And at the end of our road we have discovered that the now puckered and rutted snowmobile track is really a paved walking and biking lane that runs the full length of the some four blocks of the town. We even saw the pastor's daughters out horseback riding in the lane a few days ago.

In one week's time we have also encountered a literal abundance of new animals coming into visibility all along the quickly-melting and emerging expanses of terra firma ever-so-slowly beginning to show first signs of new growth. Because so much of the exposed territory is near roads, where the sun penetrates most easily, the animals line up along the road grousing, gazing at us and the new world around them, and sometimes even taunting us by standing in the road and questioning our presence in their dining room. Since last week we have encountered two different large elk herds along the road, one to the south of us and one to the north. They were most engaged in eating and paid us little attention either time. Then two days ago, as we were driving north toward Kalispell, a large bird with a broad white saddle across its head and neck and an impressive tail-fan alighted and flew beside our car for several seconds. As we looked back when it rose away from us, we saw it was a bald eagle who, having raced us a while, decided we were unworthy partners and unworthy prey. Of the less distinguished varieties, the black birds swoop in droves through our new small yard coming forth and all over the little lake in front of us. Yesterday they kept landing in dozens on an ancient and now-defunct feeder in our yard which was left on a branch so long that it has grown up with the tree and I imagine it will never be filled again. When the dog and I go walking, they also fly over us in a very teasing way inspecting us carefully again and again.

The deer deserve their own paragraph. They have emerged into the world in the thousands. They grouse here and there, wander about and stare. The winter deer were busy and serious and watchful, but the spring deer are leisurely and playful and unconcerned. Now when we go for walks on the logging road, the deer stand their ground and glare at us as if to say, "Still here? Don't you people have anything to do in your lives?" It is an insulting look, a look of disdain and disbelief. And the flies. Where do they come from? "Out of nowhere, out of the dark, cold world came flies." They buzz here and there filling our eyes and ears. If they weren't so pesky, they would be remarkable with their resilience. The dogs watch them buzz around until their eyes become crossed and they jolt here and there trying to catch them. Only the flies think that chase is a fun game. The dogs exhaust themselves with fly worries. And the deer flinch and bite to rid themselves of such peskiness.

In one week's time also the town itself has changed. It is almost as if this were a tent city that was set up from one minute to the next. The Gold Rush has started, the miners have started pouring in, and storefronts are shooting up here and there like a stake-out on the lookout for claim-jumpers. The activity is rather frenzied. Two real estate offices have opened after being boarded up all winter. We first noticed their neon signs in the window, then saw the agent wiping down the windows and waving at people passing by as if they were his long-lost cousins. An eager beaver at work, he also took out a full-page ad in last week's paper saying, "Hello, I'm back, and I am looking to list your property!" Neighbors two doors down have already caught his fly and put up a tin sign in their yard saying, "For Sale." We went to the post office at 10:00 Tuesday and at

10:15 this new lawn ornament was there. I wonder if they want to move or if they are just seeing what kind of offer they might get. The other real estate office is less energetic. They have turned on their sign and are making smoke in the chimney, but nothing else besides that appears to be happening. I suspect their action is "behind wraps." Perhaps they will have an ad next week for more discriminating sellers after the eager beavers and desperados fall for the first guy.

All along the main road entering town is an enormous snow-filled meadow. During the winter some of the clients at the Western Wannabe Lodge took sleigh rides across the area, while we and the locals slowed down on the road to watch them. I assumed it was an open area meant to frame the Western Wannabe Lodge so all cowhands, dudes, and sportsmen could be sufficiently buffered from the mundane, if anything about this place can be considered mundane. But earlier this week we saw big excavating machines and what-looked-like mowers out on the snowmounds and then suddenly appeared putting greens speckled across the meadow like green oases in a sea of white. Every day a little more of the driving range appears as people work in the meadow now instead of sleighing. Eventually they will be strolling and carting there, I guess, after a day of fly fishing and big game hunting and telling tall tales. And the locals will still drive slowly down the main road and watch.

Marjorie M. Snipes

Highway Elk

Friday, March 15: (39°F, low, mostly cloudy; 43°F, high)

Holidays have their own meanings in Montana. The smaller the holiday, the bigger and more lavish the celebration. It is delightful, confusing, and frustrating all at once as you want to participate in things but find there are too many and they each require choices you are not prepared to make.

So far we have seen two of these: Valentine's Day and St. Patrick's Day. (President's Day and National Pie Day did not garner much notice.) On Valentine's Day, every restaurant-saloon-casino in our area had specials as strange and extravagant as dedicating a whole day to love. Our local newspaper started advertising two weeks in advance and warning that reservations would be required at every one of the five establishments in town and around the surrounding area. Each one posted a special menu in the newspaper with lots of hearts and cupids drawn around the advertisements. On the days leading up to Valentine's every store, restaurant-saloon-casino, library, school, post office, and gas station had hearts stuck in windows to join in on the festivities. When that Thursday arrived, we anxiously wondered if we would be able to maintain our weekly pizza schedule. Our Thursdays are usually spent eating the best-pizza-on-earth at The Hungry Bear Restaurant-Bar-Casino, but they had advertised all over the Valley about their Valentine's Day Whole Broiled Lobster Plate, so I reasonably assumed that there would be no room at the inn, and even if there were, they would not want to make an $18 vegetarian pizza for three people while broiling lobster at $35 a plate in a dining room with only ten tables and a maximum seating capacity of 45. So I called the local Western Wannabe lodge, which sponsors weekly pizza nights Tuesdays through Thursdays and asked if we could make a reservation for pizza more locally. The lady who answered the phone announced, "It is Valentine's Day!" I said, "Yes, it is!" not sure where this was going. "We don't serve pizza on Valentine's Day!" she said, as if speaking to the village idiot. Chagrined, but now more knowledgeable, at first I despaired that we would have to break our ritual. But, alas, I broke down and called "The Bear" directly and asked them if they would let us come for our pizza even though they were serving much higher-classed fare that evening. The lady who answered laughed at first, surely aware of who was calling the moment I asked if they would please make us a vegetarian pizza that night and…would we be allowed to eat it in the dining room? "Come on!" she said. "We'll make room for you."

So at 5:15 we arrived at The Hungry Bear, hungry for pizza. We actually sat in our normal place (the best seat in the house right under a huge antelope on the wall), while they seated other customers around us. By 6:00 the place was full and enough lobster had passed through for me to wonder if Maine would ever recover its lobster beds. There were two waitresses that evening, and our normal waitress/cook/bartender stayed in the kitchen making lobster plates and vegetarian pizza. They brought out plastic sour cream buckets for the lobster shells, and we watched (trying to be unobtrusive) as people not at all accustomed to this crustacean, stared at it, tapped it, squeezed it in unlikely places, and then tore into it not sure what joys they were supposed to be experiencing. Most people were paired off, but at one of the nine tables there was an older man with his wife and teenage daughter. They all had lobster plates.

Now what makes this story interesting is not really the lobster, although that was certainly an attention-getter. What was interesting to me is that The Hungry Bear never has any customers in the restaurant on Thursdays. Well, I won't exaggerate…some Thursdays a forest ranger comes right at

5:00 and sits by the exit table reading a book and eating a bacon cheeseburger. Then two Thursdays ago a mother and her two children came for hamburgers and sat at the table beside us, the one under the bear head, but they could not get any service. They sat for about ten minutes and then asked us if the restaurant was open. Chewing on a hot, delicious slice of vegetarian pizza, I turned and stared, confused as to why someone would ask this question while I chewed on a fresh pizza, but then I realized they had not received menus. I told the lady, "Well, usually it is just us and that ranger over there. I guess the waitress is in the bar now, because she wasn't expecting you." I poked my son and he ran into the bar to get her. (The bar, by the way, *always* has customers.)

So back to the story of Valentine's Day...we were shocked to see every table full at "The Bear." We sat and watched the lobsters emerge from the kitchen and then out came the big round pan and the steaming vegetarian pizza with mixed cheese oozing over the sides. I had to restrain myself from clapping as my eyes became fixated on my addiction. And one-by-one the lobster clients turned their heads to follow that pan from the kitchen to our table. And the man seated in front of us said quite loudly, "Whoa, we should have ordered that." I said, "You should have. It tastes really good and is a whole lot easier to eat."

Well, this weekend is St. Patrick's Day...and here we go again. Here in Montana the thoughts of love and genetic ancestry are big. All over our town are green shamrocks and leprechauns hanging in windows and plastic-posted on store fronts. And the newspaper started two weeks ago advertising dinner specials on Sunday for corned beef and cabbage. Even the Senior Center is having a town meal and asking that everyone attend, young and old alike. There is a "Race to the

Pot O' Gold" starting at the elementary school, and parades in every city surrounding us. Like Valentine's Day, I'm beginning to feel anxious. The prospect of so much celebration is overwhelming. In Georgia we just have Savannah with its antics on St. Patrick's Day. There they just have a parade and then turn the Savannah River green. It's mild stuff compared to here. On the news this morning they announced details about the state parade in Butte, where the governor and lieutenant governor will be marching. (By the way, Butte is not the capital of Montana.) The parade announcer warned "all Montanans" that the firefighters and search-and-rescue would be in and along the parade route "trying to be of service." He said they were asking that people not bring glass bottles with them and to try to keep the backpacks and coolers as small as possible "so you don't run into other people and have accidents. And right after the parade," he said, "go down to the Starlight Bowling Lanes where the Shillelagh will be held!" Wow. We're hoping to run the "Race to the Pot O' Gold" here in our small town in record time so we can head down to Butte. It's a long way, but I bet it'd be worth the journey.

Montana Winter Days

Restaurant Trophies

Saturday, March 16: (34°F, low, misty and drizzling; 47°F, high)

We discovered a primordial world yesterday, one of those dream forests where the trees are high, there is lots of "long-haired lady" growth in the branches (epiphytes), the forest floor is clear and laden only with pine needles and large trunks, and the view is stunning. At least we think it was a stunning view – we haven't gotten to see it in slow motion yet. We had heard that this was a place where our dogs could run off-leash, but since we are such poorly-trained owners, we would never trust our dogs off leash, so we decided two things: (1) it must be dog-friendly as a park and (2) since there is no barrier saying "closed" and no patrol car anywhere, it must be open, even if it is unplowed and appears shuttered up for the season. So off we went - my mother and me.

At first we parked rather hesitantly on the side of the road and watched for glimpses of our car as we trudged away into the forest, dogs pulling with the greatest excitement of their sheltered lives. Previously they had only known established walks and nice, well-trimmed and maintained parks. They knew this adventure was wild and hairy from the get-go. Entering this world of snow and ice, from a town that had emerged substantially from winter, it was compelling. The dogs pulled us up to trunks that were clearly rubbed by some wild animal. At times we were treeing the scent of varmints and at other times we were pulled willy-nilly and then underneath a large ponderosa crossing our path. It took a hunk of time to get enough control of them that we could navigate in some kind of pretentious forward motion. It took about an hour. Luckily the trail area was well marked and sometimes cleared, as it intersected at one point with a boating ramp on the lake put to all-season use for fishing. For the duration of the walk the dogs remained highly animated, but we were increasingly in control as they slowed to a soft trot, now zigzagging from one tree on the left side that smelled promising to one right over on the other side equally alluring. Needless to say, we saw no wildlife. Even the flies stayed away from the rushing storm of noise and tumult we brought along with us.

In the end, as we saw our car re-emerge in front of us, thankful that this frenetic hike had still produced a large circle in the forest, we saw that we had been gone just a bit under two hours and proved that "all's well that ends well." We gave the dogs some water at the car and they heaved themselves in with some trouble as they were worn out from their wild adventure. Both were asleep before I turned the ignition. We headed back into town, stopped for a coffee at the gas station, retrieved the mail, and headed back to the cabin. And as with most things that are wildly emotional, we began to forget the feeling of being dragged through the forest, grazing trees head-on, fumbling over downed trunks, and twirling dizzily. We kept talking about the beauty and exhilaration of it all.

So at 3:00 I picked up my son from school and we went to the church to practice piano. Tired and beginning to feel sore, I still kept to our strict piano practice schedule and my son and I discussed only wrong notes, wrong fingering, weak dynamics, and an unconvincing tremolo on the boogie woogie. Then the practice ended and we went to the car. This is the time when we actually began telling each other about our respective days. He started and I heard about shepherd's pie for lunch ("Mama, have you ever heard of a pie made with potatoes and meat and no sugar?"), playing "four-square" at recess, the new mythology book he checked out from the library for the weekend, and the dirty gym clothes I had to wash before Sunday's "Race to the Pot O' Gold."

Then it was my turn. "Well, we went on a hike (I still used that euphemism) in a magical forest." "With the dogs, Mama? Did everyone make it? Were you scared? Did you see any leprechauns? Did the bears chase you?" I fielded question after question, sensing my own thrill to share this place with him rising by the second. By now it was 4:30 p.m. Without thinking anything rational, I blurted out, "If we hurry, we can go back and make a quick loop before it gets dark!" "Yea, Mama, let's go! I'll protect you from the bears this time!"

We drove up to the cabin and I waked my mother from her stupor only to say, "We're going back." She didn't need any more information than that. "Right now?" she asked, horrified. "Yes!" I said. My mother, ever the trooper and clearly a source of my own DNA, someone who would prefer to be in the woods on a wild adventure than sheltered, warm, and bored, got up and started lacing up high-top snow boots in a rote manner. Then she announced, "I'm not taking Brave back with me this time. He's had enough." No doubt. Whatever it was that he had, he had definitely had enough. He was on his back, legs splayed out, snoring. Kalispell, however, had gone for her own leash and was nudging at the door. She was sure she could get that varmint this time.

So we returned, except this time some things were different: we parked the car on the side of the road without ever looking back (it was now, after all, a private parking place), we dodged trees more effectively this time (the dog was still tired from the morning), and my son kept looking at our earlier tracks and asking, "Why did you go that way? Why do your tracks stop right there in front of that tree, Mama? Mama, why did you lay down there? There are more tracks, Mama, way over there!" So we avoided our earlier tracks – uh, I mean trail – and forged on new lands. It was more beautiful, more intense this time because we saw the forest and the trees as we tromped at a nice clip.

What a world.... every day we wake up a refreshed Corps of Discovery. What a life....something new every day. What a place....truly God's Garden. We didn't see any grizzlies yesterday, but the prospect remains.

A Wild Walk through the Wooly Woods

Sunday, March 17: (32°F, low, blustery snow; 38°F, high)

All day today our town has been experiencing a Georgia snow. Here and there and with utter abandon, exquisite crystalline flakes decked out in tutus float and frolic and pirouette on their way to the most delicate landing on their tippy toes, wherever they happen to be – on the tree branches, sidewalks, handrails, or rooftops. This snow is frivolous and wasteful, like a pair of lace-cuffed dungarees. The locals, intensely energized by the oncoming early spring and aware that

March snows are the quickest of events, and the Georgians, still snow crazy after all these weeks, are both able to thrill in this windfall and glory in the windy, slushy, glittery mess.

My son ran his race to the Pot O' Gold today. Snow has no effect on Montanans. None at all. We ate lunch with some dear local friends right before the start of the race, watching literal snow showers pour outside and pelt the windows, and I queried and quarried them in their wisdom saying, "This race today is really another joke, isn't it? I mean, no one actually has foot races in the snow and ice." And they looked at me with great concern and befuddlement, devoid of any amusement, "Today's race is a real race. They will be running for their best times." "But those will be snow times, no?" I asked. "I don't think it matters about the weather. It's just a race like any other." "Really? Are you kidding me?" I said. Now thoroughly alarmed, "But what will they wear on their feet? Will they race in snow boots, hats, and coats?" After all, my son had his snow boots on his feet at that moment. "Well," they considered the oddity of my question, "I guess they will run in whatever footwear they usually use to run. We don't really think of the snow as a special condition." Don't think of the snow as a special condition? Really?

We left our friends in what I thought was their very sheltered life and arrived three blocks down the road at the Race Headquarters housed inside the elementary school. And there they were - Usain Bolts in tight race wear that clung to the arms and legs, running shoes, and huge jumbo numbers on their mid-quarters. I almost swallowed my tongue. Their only concession to the reality of the real world was a skin-tight ski cap pulled over their heads. I mean, not even gloves. So I checked to see if the pavement would allow upright or prone movement and then agreed my son could wear his running shoes if he intended to be competitive at all, but he also had on blue jeans, a ski jacket, gloves, and a hat. He was the only runner with his jumbo-tron numbers pinned on a coat. As the Start neared, little kids got up on the front line for the one kilometer "Fun Run" and the "serious" racers (who apparently are not allowed any fun at all) got behind – first the 5k-ers and then the 10k-ers. I stayed aside of the whole group peering intently to see my son through the blizzard. Pistol went off, runners started, and my son shrugged his shoulders and lit out like a Georgia firecracker. By the time he got 15 yards away he was invisible in the snowstorm. So I repositioned myself at the next block beside the water guy with bottles and a huge tank of Gatorade. I laughed and told him I bet he wouldn't have much work today, as who would want water in freezing temperatures and blizzard conditions? He looked at me strangely like I was from Georgia or something and said, "Runners always need water." OK, and they need snow boots, a ski jacket, and headlights, too, I thought to myself. Just then, my son started coming into view through the mist and snow, and the race organizers craned to see who was in the lead for the Fun Run division. One man started laughing and said, "Look at the leader! He's wearing a coat!"

Marjorie M. Snipes

On Your Mark!

Monday, March 18: (24°F, low, heavy snow all day; 32°F, high)

I think this is called respite, a time when you receive a brimming measure so that it pours over the sides, a baker's dozen, if you will, a cup running over, *yapa*. Last night we got more than three inches of beautiful, glorious snow. It is collected on everything visible – branches, electric wires, rooftops, and even the most tender little shoots of grass, which can be seen now. And little by little winter is erasing spring today. They are in their own foot race and today the heat goes to winter. The world is black and white and has lost all color and our neighbors have disappeared again. The only things in movement this morning besides the school bus at 7:25 are deer. Two or three at a time, they cross our yard slowly, ambling, grousing, and nudging at the snow, at home once more in this quieter world.

I sit at my table looking out, snow falling thickly, and I feel such contentment that it draws up tears and melancholia. For this moment, at this time, right now, all is so right with the world. It is Edenic and I feel in place at last, watching the most gorgeous scene imaginable right in front of me. If I lived here permanently, I wonder what I would see. But I am a passerby, alas, a sojourner, and this place and this time are borrowed. For once I deeply see the gift I have been given.

It is snowing again. Maybe if I try hard enough I can make the calendar move backward again like the weather.

Tuesday, March 19: (19°F, low, partly cloudy; 43°F, high)

The snow did not even begin to diminish until well after dusk yesterday, and this morning the world is stunned and heavy-laden with a great burden of beauty. I walked the dog out onto the logging road, but she wouldn't go more than ten yards before reversing and pulling me back towards the cut-through to our cabin. At first she looked for the path, bounding through the snow, but then she realized there was no path, only deep snow everywhere, some eight inches blanketing every surface. She decided that we should wait until a snowmobile passed so that we had ruts for walking.

I certainly understand her preference. It is hard work to walk in deep snow. In fact, last weekend we went on a forest walk to see a tree with a proper name. Two different people have told us we *must* go to see this tree. So we went after lunch, parked the car in the middle of the road, and got out to walk through the forest area they had indicated to seek "Gus." "Oh," one of the men said with disdain, when I asked him how far it is from the road, "it is just 50 yards from the road." OK. But I should have asked, "How long does it take to traverse those 50 yards?" This is kind of like in the Andes when I would ask them how far someone's farm was from the river. "Uyy," they would say, "no more than a kilometer." And then I would take off expecting a 15-minute walk and arrive two hours later, exhausted from a 1000-foot climb and descent over Mt. Everest.

Well, we worked at getting to Gus for about 20 minutes and then gave up from fear. At one point, I was in the snow up to my thighs and had to work deftly to extricate one of my boots from the snowfield. I never stepped where snow did not at least reach right at my knees. Not able to find the trail, just extraneous markers located literally level with our knees here and there telling about the culture of the local Native Americans who lived in the area and some famous forest fires that had passed through this spot, something ludicrous to fathom while sinking in snow, I decided that the prospect of finding the tree in a straight line was too slim to warrant any further search. After getting about 15 yards from the road, we crawled and clawed our way back to the road. Gus will have to wait till another time for our introduction. I have decided to set voluntary limits on snow-walking: six inches. That sounds fair. Once it exceeds six inches, I swivel backward and "leave no trace."

Wednesday, March 20: (18°F, low, cloudy, then snow, sleet, wind; 55°F, high)

I remain amazed at this place. This time I mean "place" in a larger sense of the word. Every morning I listen to Missoula country radio. I listen to the country station because it is the only FM station I can get. So, little by little, I've gotten "hip" with the latest country songs and crooners, who is seeing whom, what is happening on the Nashville scene, what the country pop charts say this week, and what Missoula thinks about it all. I also get the treat of hearing locally-produced commercials, call-ins from every Tom, Dick, and Harry, upcoming events, and sports announcements. Always sports. And now during March Madness, this is almost all I hear.

So we live here in the Valley, but Missoula is also part of our turf, if you will. And because of the radio, I feel connected and up-to-date with Missoula events, perhaps more than my own town in Georgia. And what I have heard about over these many weeks of radio-listening is that the culture of communality that I have experienced here in our town is also something they do in Missoula.

This morning the announcers told us about a fire that had destroyed the shop of a well-known mechanic there. They mentioned his business and his name as if everyone knew him and knew about the tragedy and that the date for the fund-raising auction was next week sometime. They mentioned several area businesses that were donating for the auction and asked others to bring by anything they had to add to it as well. "The goal," they said, "is to get him back on his feet right away. We know that with your help we can raise enough money to get his business rebuilt and his equipment replaced."

What kind of community does this kind of sharing build? What is the result of the accumulation of actions in giving to each other on the large-scale as a group, not just to "my" school or "my" church or "my" friend? What ends up if we give to someone not as if it were a charity case for sympathy, but a "class-action" responsibility to preserve, rebuild, and recover?

Well, these questions are too big to answer in theory, but in fact they can be answered. I wonder if this type of spirit got going as an attribute of living in an area where everyone must rely upon themselves and their neighbors to survive. I wonder if this is not the result of living in a place where everyone's skills are valued and irreplaceable so that if the mechanic decided he'd been defeated and would "go back East" (a euphemism surely of having failed), then everyone would lose, not just a friend and neighbor, but a mechanic who was good and capable and...irreplaceable. I also see what ends up here...something basic and good and kind. It isn't that we don't have this where I live – again I think about my neighbors who came to mop up my garage after the water heater broke two months ago without me ever having asked them. We also take care of our own, give freely and without question, and bond together in commitment to each other; but because our places are so big and so populous, we have less sense of meaning in the whole. We live invested deeply in our community, but it is not defined on the widest geographical scale because that scale is too big to begin with. That changes things essentially.

Population changes things. The sheer numbers of people who exist in an area changes things. While here, from time to time, I have gotten an e-mail invitation for some event in Atlanta that draws me. The Atlanta Opera sends me notices about various events I am missing; the Fox Theater sends notices about upcoming plays and revues I have missed; and even my own University sends occasional announcements about lectures, theater productions, and concerts that happened while I was here. I missed those things. I miss those things. That is also part of who I am and those are the benefits of population. I can listen to Uncle Louie's washtub band or attend a New York City opera group performing "La Traviata" if I am there. I can also be loved by my own group and my circles. But if I am here, in exchange for the opera, I get a world of connection to each other and absolutely everyone, learning to appreciate people and things to which I might not have first gravitated. Some days I think that is a greater gain than Giuseppe Verdi.

Thursday, March 21: (28°F, low, snow then partly cloudy; 46°F, high)

I left my son at his school today. Just left him and never picked him up. In fact, I didn't even think about picking him up.

You see, on Thursdays the children have "early out." In fact, Thursday is called, "Early Out Thursday." They go to school at the same time every morning and return home every day by the clock. Except on Thursdays. On Thursdays they go to school at the same time, but they get out of school one hour early. This delights both children and faculty enormously and bothers pretty much all parents, as it means that schedules shift in the middle of the week.

I knew about this in theory. In fact, I was warned about "Early Out Thursdays" when we first showed up at the school. But because my son joined Nordic skiing on Thursdays as soon as he got here, we actually experienced "Very Late Thursdays." Instead of getting out at 2:00, he got out at 4:30 p.m. This meant that for us Thursdays were long school days, not short ones. And then when skiing ended three weeks ago, he joined After School Fitness that began to meet on that day as well. Anyhow, this Thursday the fitness was cancelled and so, in my mind, we simply had to pick him up when school ended, and, for me, school ended at 3:00 as it did on Mondays, Tuesdays, Wednesdays, and Fridays.

At 2:30 p.m. I was walking my dog when Pastor drove up our hill in his truck. I was delighted to see him, although it was not the first time he had visited us. He and his son had visited us a few weeks earlier when our car skidded into the snowbank beside our driveway because I didn't "gun it" enough to get over the sheet of ice at the top of the driveway. That day we began a rapid descent backwards and then slowed a bit as we figure-eighted into the mound of snow (now ice) scraped from the driveway earlier in the season. We were left half-way up the driveway in the wrong position to ever think we might get out on our own. That was on a Wednesday. I called him. Well, actually, I called the mechanic in town, but he didn't answer his phone, so since Pastor knows everyone in town, I called him second. He laughed at me and said he'd see what he could do. Within 10 minutes he was in the driveway with a huge chain and he and his son began attaching it to the two vehicles. He told me to get in my car and try to steer it in neutral, "but keep your foot off the brake."

Well, there are times in life when we can think voluntarily and other times when instinct takes over. For the first two pulls of the car, I stabbed the brakes with all my might as soon as it started moving backwards. Ever-patient Pastor stopped two times, got out of his truck, and asked me kindly to not press the brakes. Tears streaming down my face as I anticipated this ending in total destruction of both vehicles, I asked what I would do if I started careening right into his truck. He looked at me with a tired compassion and said, "We are not going fast, no one will get hurt, and as far as the vehicles, that's why we have insurance." There is an important lesson here, although I didn't fully get it until my mother and I relived the events a few hours later after the adrenaline passed. What is the point of taking care of ourselves and others, our property and our lives if, in the moment in which we most need fearlessness, we are not willing to grab on to that courage with confidence? This is a lesson that I need time to ponder – over and over again. Well, so, clearly we all lived through that first visit of Pastor, so this time I waved and greeted him warmly, thinking that he was here to just say "hello!"

He said, "Hello! How are you?" and I started talking about the weather, my walk with the dog, and what we would be doing on Sunday. He listened, ever patient as always. And then, about 10 minutes into the surprise visitation, he asked if I was heading over to the school to pick up Joseph. "Yes! I'll leave in about 15 minutes," I said. "Well," he said, "that is why I came by. Today they got out early and he is waiting for you right now. He called me to come get you." "Oh!" I screamed, hysterical yet again. I shoved Kalispell into the car, screamed for my mother to bring the keys, and started crying. And he started laughing again. He said, "It's alright. We all forget them sometimes. He's safe at the school."

When I got there, my son was all alone in the office, tears were brimming, and he asked, "Did you forget about me, Mama?" Early Outs....definitely not all fond memories for us.

Friday, March 22: (9°F, low, windy and occasional snow; 37°F, high)

Tonight was the Dutch Supper in Manhattan, an event we have anticipated for seven years. No kidding. The proper name, though, is Dutch Supper and Tulip Mania Auction, and it is the annual fund raiser and benefit for the K-12 Manhattan Christian School located just a few miles northwest of Bozeman, Montana in a community first settled by Dutch pioneers. We first attended in 2006, after reading a book on unique and quirky things to do in Montana, a book that shockingly had a beginning and end to it, and we were amazed at the numbers of people who materialized seemingly in the middle of nowhere!

There were lines to park (and parking all over the fields surrounding the school), lines to buy tickets (and people focused intently on making sure they got one), lines to enter the old gymnasium (lines that meandered for what appeared to be miles throughout the school and along the students' lockers), lines to get plates and food (and tables scattered everywhere into "food stations"). And at each of the seven Food Stations, there were signs in Dutch mockingly identifying the foods....*snert, aardappel soep, saucijzebroodjes, pot eten, poffert, stamppot van kool, boterkoek* and dozens of pastries that made your mouth water and your mind wander! Then, at the exit area, there was a "Dutch store," where they sold paraphernalia associated with the school and lots of handmade items from the surrounding community.

All of us intrepid eaters sat together at family-style tables, announcing to each other what foods we liked, didn't like, and (always) how much fun this was. We took pictures of each other, the foods, the gym, and then lots of pictures of the children's clogging groups who came out in their massive wooden shoes, rhythmically clanging across the stage area to entertain our eyes and warm our hearts, as the food warmed our bellies. It was an evening we never forgot and always wanted to repeat.

This time, seven years later, it was and was not quite the same - there were those inimitable changes…again. A new gym, a huge parking lot, a bigger Dutch store, and a much better-organized Food Station area. In fact, the pastry section had become so bloated that it was moved into another area of the school, along with the cloggers. We had lots of fun. It was well worth the three and one-half hour drive to get there. But the disorganization of the early years, when the event clearly exceeded the organizers' wildest hopes and left everyone scrambling to get in and participate, was also a lost blessing. That first messy simplicity, exchanged for progress, left us without a discoverer and explorer mentality and made us more sedate in participating. We enjoyed it, but it wasn't "the same." Success might be better an aspiration than an accomplishment. I must think about this some more.

Saturday, March 23: (14°F, low, partly sunny, windy, occasional snow showers; 36°F, high)

Well, I confess that today I could be officially charged with "going Montanan." It was not one thing that caused it, but a combination of circumstances and coincidences. I'm glad it happened, really, because it was the most fun I've ever had. We got up early, packed our saddlebags, and headed east to Great Falls, dogs on board, gas tank half empty, and no maps. The "Made in Montana" show was open for the public at the Civic Center, so I headed to the center of town, where I would expect to find a Civic Center, and there it was. Clearly, these city planners were in a class of their own. Not only were things exactly where their names said they should be, but I could make left turns anywhere and everywhere I wanted.

But before I extol the virtues of driving map-less in Great Falls too much, do know that I eventually encountered a potentially bigger problem for the uninitiated: every street is numbered, no matter what direction it runs, as if names themselves were simply too much to bear for the Great Falleans. So, roads going east-west (and there are bunches of them) are numbered north and south and called "avenues" and roads going north and south are numbered east and west and called "streets." So, if you are looking for the 400-block of 4th street, then you need to go to the corner of 4th St and 4th Ave. My head was spinning, as I tried to remember which came first and in which direction because after attending the Show, and eating ourselves senseless on buffalo jerky from the Fort Belknap booth, we decided we should go to the Charlie Russell Museum. "Well, that is on 13th and 4th," they said. Say what? Which is first, avenue or street? Is 13th and 4th the same as 4th and 13th? Well we got there, with no rhyme or reason, and saw a big sign posted on the door that said, "Free Admission Today!" Ahoy! What luck! So we trudged up to the door thinking that we had hit the jackpot, only to find out that a large amount of the works were not there and that is why admission was free. "Not here?" I asked. "No, we took them out for an auction, so there isn't much left." Say what? Kind of like going to the Louvre to see the Mona Lisa and finding out that it was missing because they took it out for a garage sale.

Now I may not be so sophisticated that I could blend in with the crowd in New York City, but I have walked some avenues myself and this didn't sound right. I mean, I know auctions are important in Montana, but why the heck would you remove the contents of a world-famous museum to take it on a stroll to an auction? And what did they do? Did they auction off the Russells there? Why would you auction off the contents of a museum to raise money for the museum? Well, in the end, it seems they took a lot of paintings to decorate some other place where they were auctioning off other stuff. Oh, OK, so the museum emptied its contents for an interior design booth at the local hotel conference center? Maybe so. I haven't figured that one out yet. But we walked around the bison exhibit downstairs and then out to the little log cabin studio where Russell painted so many of the missing masterpieces we did not see.

Then we headed out of town to Ulm, a little place that amounts to almost nothing on the map – well, nothing on our map, as we didn't have one. I remembered it being south of town, so we headed that way and found the exit about seven miles later. But before you think I mean that Ulm amounts to nothing, let me assure you that Ulm is not just a place, it is a legacy. We went through the little settlement and out to the buffalo jump, Ulm Pishkun. You can see it from every direction on the landscape, a true Place. The ranger there told us to feel free to walk our dogs on the trail, so we piled out, leashed up our unruly dogs, and headed up to the plateau of the Jump, covered thickly with prairie dogs. We had to dodge other Montanans with their dogs – I mean what is a Montanan without a dog? It was cold, and wind so fierce it could carve out lines on your face, and views so stunning that they pulled you down to your knees. We took very inadequate pictures, but the memory is etched forever in our vision of this magnificent landscape. "Big Sky" goes nowhere near a proper description. I personally think Montana should change its nickname to "Wow!"

And then as if buffalo jerky, auctions, and dogs were not Montanan enough, we headed back towards our Valley after descending the Jump, trying desperately to get to a restaurant-bar-casino before the NCAA Women's playoffs Montana-Georgia game began. Now I have never been a basketball aficionado, but since coming to Montana, I got converted. We had heard about this playoff game for over a week, and the Montanans were in high form of excitement over their Lady Griz making it to the tournament and facing such an unwarranted rival as Georgia. During his last week in school, my son had heard nothing but taunts and challenges from the locals who no longer found his home state so amusing. After he learned about the Georgia team from the locals here, he had handled it gracefully when they said that the "Lady Griz will maul those Bulldogs!"

So we had gotten across the plains and to the foot of the Rockies when the Big Game started. Fumbling quickly at the hour it was to start, we got it on AM radio and listened until Rodgers Pass, when the reception changed and then Dolly Parton started crooning about her coat of many colors. At the time of communication loss, the score was 32-30, Georgia ahead by two. Uyy. We hurtled down the Pass setting land-speed records to rival Bonneville Flats, no one else on the road anywhere, and made it to Lincoln at the beginning of the last quarter. First, we stopped at the Shake N' Burger. I ran in to see if they had a television going, but they didn't. The waitress, deeply sympathetic, told me to go to the Bootleggers' Bar, that they had lots of TVs. Well, so, we drove the block down the road and pulled into an establishment that looked like it was founded by Lewis and Clark and where every client had a truck huddled at the door. I initially flinched, my whole upbringing momentarily asserting itself to try to save me, but, alas, I overrode every caution and grabbed the hand of my 10 year-old on one side and my 70+ year-old mother, and we walked through that door boldly, strode up to the bar, where we found three stools with our names on them in front of a TV. Best food we've had in Montana, except for The Hungry Bear. And the taste of the food got better and better as the game wrapped up. What a thing it was to sit at the Bootleggers with all of the others, watching a women's basketball game, in a little town where they apprehended the Unabomber, halfway home on our side of the mountain. These are the moments of our lives that embed themselves in our long-term memory. So, if some time, probably not too many years from now, I start losing my faculties and you hear me say, "What's the score?" you'll know. You'll know.

By the way, I won't say the score again. But we did walk out of that joint with our heads high, betting that Montanans won't be adopting bulldogs any time soon, though. I expect they've had enough of them for now.

It was a beautiful thing all over. As we made our way back to the cabin, within legal speed limits now, we passed deer and elk and the most gut-wrenching scenes of what can only be called awesome beauty, forgetting all human things and remembering that we are sojourners here in a Garden of Eden.

Burgers and Basketball in a Bar

Sunday, March 24: (10°F, low, sunny; 37°F high)

How to say goodbye is one of the most difficult tasks we face as individuals. Sometimes the scenario demands that we do it at a specific time, but other times it drags on. Attachment is a very sticky thing and involves our church family, our school family, a music teacher, a librarian, and a waitress at The

Hungry Bear. Departure is a ritual. It should be done right or it changes everything.

    A former student wrote me today to say that her mother is dying. I feel such compassion for her, having lost my own father nine years ago. These two things, goodbyes and death, are hardly comparable, yet they do seem to share certain aspects of each other. Both are forms of loss that deepen as we age – we carry them more heavily as we get older; both require us to redefine ourselves in ways that initially threaten to diminish us – they force change upon us; and both leave us wondering, will we ever see each other again? On good days, on confident days, most of us carry this longing and grief well, but on dark days we can stumble.

    Each goodbye has its own shape and dimension, and while I can talk eloquently about those we know best and why leaving them hurts so much, it is those we have known *least* who mostly catch my attention. How can I make sense of this? How can someone whose name I do not even know cause me grief similar in kind to that of my dearest friends?

    I have been thinking about this for a while now, as we have discussed our last Thursday night at The Hungry Bear. Everyone in my little family felt the same way I did: How do we say goodbye? How do we properly acknowledge that this little weekly dinner ritual shaped our lives in the most delightful way? How do we express gratitude for something so intangible as a smile, a weekly greeting, the beauty (yes, beauty) of someone knowing what we liked to eat and drink and remembering that from week to week? One of my dearest friends in life was my minister during college and later my mentor and friend. He always told me, "Simple grace is God's deepest bounty." I wonder if this makes sense here. I think that those with whom we connect on a deeply spiritual plane – those who seem to understand us without words and without assurances – are likely those with whom we have a relationship of simple grace. It goes without saying. And it goes deep.

On our last night at The Hungry Bear, we left a card and a small token gift to say "thank you" to our waitress, chef, and friend whose name we did not know. When she passed by the table for the last time, we gave this to her and then asked her name – and she asked ours. We hugged each other. It was poignant and meaningful. She left to attend a customer at the bar and we gathered our things and began to leave "The Bear" for the last time. But as we passed by the bar area to the parking lot, she emerged once more and we hugged each other once again. Too often I think we forget to consider that what is deeply meaningful for us is very likely shared with the other as well. Sometimes I think we should be more forthright with each other and delight in that fact; but other times, like this one, that slow accumulation of meaning over weeks of rather mundane and routine interactions, was more profound because it appeared freely and un-orchestrated. Truly, grace.

As humans, we are all actors in complicated lives where we try to direct and manage the course of events, yet we also interact and invest in each other repeatedly and quite innocently, without thinking. We go about our day-to-day lives seeking services, helping others, stopping to do something we were not asked, and not thinking that these somewhat hidden acts and dramas that rarely rise to the level of undivided attention may be our most significant human acts. When we discover grace in hidden places and in each other's hearts – true grace that was not earned or sought – we feel a sense of meaning and purposefulness that revives our spirits and reminds us that there very well may be a lot more going on than we can know. The life that happens around us, unplanned and uncontrolled, is potentially as deep as, *if not deeper than*, the life we "make." That is a soothing thought to me.

Monday, March 25: (19°F, low, partly cloudy; 52°F, high)

    Why do we leave before we've left? There is something about attachment that makes us want to flee when the time comes. Time and the mind are enemies. Since yesterday, now one week from the end of this marvelous adventure, the anticipation of leaving has become palpable enough that I have begun to have dreams of just packing and going in the middle of the night. It isn't just the rituals of saying goodbye, although those loom large and fearfully in front of us, it is also that we can no longer plan forward from here and now. I am temporarily stuck considering the magnitude of packing a small car with three people, two dogs, and two cats, and the accumulations of a school semester of work for two of us and the many sundry gatherings we have made in our life in this place.

    I have also begun thinking about our return route, carrying the burden of finding a safe weather route (since snow is predicted for large areas of the Rockies), somewhat efficient mileage (since the cats do not enjoy traveling), and yet a plan that takes us through areas we are eager to see. I am wise enough to know that the shortest route may not be the best when it comes to breaking ties in one place and then entering some four days of transition time before arriving home. So I am now caught up in considering Antelope Island, Arches National Park, and Sand Creek National Historic Site. How to travel, how to break up days, new goals to set – this is the agenda for this week. Something must pull us for us to go from here well at heart because nothing will push us from here. That is for sure. Our roots are now too deep.

And so, while in place, I am distracted from being here. It started yesterday. Once people begin telling you goodbye, you start to leave, whether or not it is time. It is not brusque, it is not rude, but it is definitive. Just as the ice is breaking here and there in the larger lakes, so also are our friendships and familiarities. Something about life. We look ahead. Always aware of now and forecasting what is to come. Once people around you can no longer see you ahead, things start to fray thread by thread, and the seams, so taut throughout this winter, begin to loosen, piece by piece.

And so I have found that being here every day, all day, is harder each day. The distraction makes me antsy and anxious. I go back to the aching fact that part of me wishes to not walk to the end, but simply to pack up and leave. After all, what good are goodbyes? What purpose do they serve besides sadness? If I were more coarse and sensible, I would gather up my little family, pack the car, and leave before sunlight, leaving a note or sending a postcard afterward.

But humans are not a sensible species. If we were there would be no attachments at all. Something propels us all – leavers and stayers – to plod through this thick sadness as if going through a dress rehearsal for those partings that are irremediable and darkest. As my student writes about her dying mother, and I share storefront wisdom, I hear her deep fears and know that I must cut my teeth on smaller losses to prepare for the larger ones. And so I stay here until the end, tears streaming down my cheeks at times as I hug someone goodbye, making conversations filled with light-hearted and meaningless banter just to connect with someone that I care for, extending invitations to my home so far away from here while we both assure each other that surely in our lifespans they will travel into my orbit and we will see each other again. And then those closest to us say "I love you" in such achingly real ways that I choke. They say, "Why don't you try to get a job here?" "Why don't you buy a tiny piece of land and start planning on coming regularly, even if from time to time? Just come and you can borrow a tent and camp out on your land." "Why don't you come this summer? You can stay in our camper right there." A lady on the lunch staff at my son's school hugged us both goodbye with tears in her eyes and when I said "Thank you for making us feel so much at home here," she responded, "But this is your home. You belong here. From the beginning I knew that." All of these words come out, but what I keep hearing is "I love you and want you to stay in our lives." And I weep at that. It is undeserved. It is *yapa,* that moment when whatever is being filled begins to spill over and grace appears.

    I suppose this is not all that much different from the beauty of the mid-Valley around The Hungry Bear that I thought about earlier. Just as I travel there and ache and pain for the beauty I see, I now experience that the greatest connection and truest human joy is also an aching sadness. I want to say that love is deeply sad, that beauty is sad, whether physical or emotional. It doesn't sound right when I read it, but I know what I mean. It is overflowing and uncontainable and calls me to render myself. And it hurts. And I must think about that some more.

Tuesday, March 26: (43°F, low, sunny; 58°F, high – in Paradise, MT)

We were on the road seeing this incredible state today. We have been traveling a lot during these last few days. After spending the night at the hot springs in Paradise, we headed back to the National Bison Range, which we had traversed yesterday en route. The sheer size of the bison is amazing. The winter driving area in the park is small but meandering and it overshadows a beautiful lowland creek area where the animals like to go for water. We had seen a bachelor group yesterday cross the road headed for the water and a wallow area nearby and had gotten some great photos. This time of year the beauty of the whole state is enhanced by the privacy of everything we do. There are virtually no other tourists anywhere we go. What few we are seem more as stragglers in the Garden of Eden who greet each other with delight. Today we took the West Loop around the area and then drove down to the picnicking area where we could take the dogs on a nature hike. The chilly sun was so wonderful and we embraced the oncoming spring in the midst of a magical secondary forest surrounding a pond filled with cattails. It was beautiful.

And as we later made our way through the Flathead Valley "of Delight," seeing scenes so unimaginably beautiful that I gave up photography and, after a while, even trying to grasp it visually – low-lying rich, golden, straw-filled valley, a large, wide glacial-blue lake so enormous it could be a small sea, and, surrounding it all on virtually every side, tall, stark white, snow-covered peaks of "these shining mountains" – it made me start thinking about beauty. "Beauty is a cultural construction" – that is what we yap about so much in anthropology. Every culture perceives the world through its own senses. Elongated necks, plucked eyebrows, tattoos, lip discs, stiletto heels...some culture somewhere finds that beautiful, while others reject it. This is not earth-shattering news.

But what about landscapes? Well, it seems that, too, is a cultural construction – from rock gardens and topiary to cleaned and brushed earth yards and well-manicured, chemically loaded green lawns to look at and not touch, and even wildscapes where the earth is left seemingly untouched, cultures define these things as appealing or not. But so often during these travels I have looked out at a valley surrounded by stunning mountains and wondered if there is also the concept of a universal beauty in landscape. I wondered today about the Native Americans who inhabited these lands long before Europeans ever got to the New World. I know they saw travail and difficulties of passage and the hunt in these mountains. But did they not also see beauty? I wonder...could a human look at these stately giants with their snowed-over peaks and not sense some sort of awe and majesty? Maybe it would be a "terrible beauty," but might the response be cross-culturally understandable? Perhaps I am awfully ethnocentric when it comes to mountains; I acknowledge that I am deeply drawn to them. But today as I drove through that fair valley, I could hear echoes of the First Peoples saying the same thing that the drummer from Arlee said so many weeks before, "Man, aren't we lucky to live in this beautiful place!"

The Wallow

Wednesday, March 27: (25°F, low, partly cloudy; 57°F, high)

Spring has definitely now won. Even in the most resistant outposts, it is strolling boldly now. When we crossed the Flathead Valley yesterday the fields were already plowed, stores that had closed for the winter had "Open for Business" signs in the windows, and people were walking about in the small towns speaking with neighbors on street corners and at mailboxes. Polson seemed transformed into a small Maine fishing village out on this broad Montana valley. Eateries had their signs out on the street with their daily specials and thrift stores had windows dressed in pastels and Easter bunnies. It was odd for us, as if someone had jumpstarted the season while we were driving here from our Valley.

Montana Winter Days

Our Valley is less ebullient about spring, more cautious, moving at the beat of its own drummer. Here in our town today, the lakes are showing a mere hint of transparency and lone ice fishermen hold out, daring the logics of physics, confident that there is one more fish with a seasonal death wish. However, they no longer take their cars with them onto the ice. Yesterday we saw only a man in an aluminum chair, a mere speck on the ice, and even he was closer to the shoreline than he had been the day before.

The deer have begun to distinguish themselves, some getting larger than others. And the birds are everywhere – blackbirds flying in hordes to grouse, small little tan and white birds pecking at stalks of newly-growing grass, and ducks of all types passing over the landscape. The Canada geese are hollering loudly, the loons are cooing their lonely strains, and even two long-necked Trumpeter swans, so achingly graceful in flight with their large bodies and aerodynamic flight pattern, are venturing out. For the smallest moment, they both flew just feet over the front of our car leading it onward like two pack mules of the sky.

The pond in front of our cabin is still frozen, but increasingly translucent. It will break soon. There is still snow fringing the edges of the white expanse. Movement is everywhere as winter retreats. But here it does so slowly, as if backing out of the doorway step by step, keeping its eyes on us from its strongholds. At first I was sad to see the retreat. The diminishment of winter signals for change. Animals (humans included) and plants begin shifting their residences. But now, more accustomed to the idea, I am readying myself for transition as well. Some sadness, some reluctance, but also some hopefulness and eagerness. It is time.

Thursday, March 28: (33°F, low, partly cloudy; 62°F, high - in Missoula, MT)

Today as we sat at breakfast, the school bus passed by our cabin. My son had gone outside to read the temperature gauge and he ducked behind a tree. It was instinctual and at first it made me laugh. Why would he hide from the bus? But when he returned I didn't ask him because I know why he hid from the bus. Our minds and our bodies are tightly entwined and braided together as one. He knows. He knows that while he is physically here a while longer, he has also already left. And so he erases himself from the pictures in which he does not belong.

As his mother, this intensifies my own emotional burden. And I resign myself to travel today – somewhere, anywhere, but we must go away for a few hours today to busy ourselves. I know he must find a place where he can be present today because here he feels absence now.

Friday, March 29: (33°F, low, mostly sunny; 60°F, high)

It is amazing that while the rest of the world around us turns spring, the lake in front of our house remains frozen and ringed with snowpack. Our town still has some snow, but our lake and immediate area seem to have the most. Meanwhile, right in front of the cabin in our little yard, grass is sprouting and new leaf buds are shimmering on the aspen trees. It is now like a diorama where the foreground is spring and the background represents a typical winter scene. Some mornings I can't decide which stage to play on, as we can now tromp through speckled forest areas in tennis shoes some days and on others we go deeper in the woods in our snow boots.

Yesterday we chose tennis shoes and played on the shoreline of the Blackfoot River. We were returning from our last trip to Missoula and passed a fishing access area right on the river. Since the snowpack has receded so dramatically, I quickly bee-lined into the little forested area so that we could go down and touch the swiftly-moving waters. The descent was rocky and a bit "trepidatious," but we moved down slowly bracing with our hands. At the bottom, my son began throwing rocks into the waters trying to skip stones on a surface of subtle breakers and spray, while I took pictures and my mother searched for the perfect stone to complete her exquisite *inuksuk* painstakingly assembled over the many weeks of travel over this beautiful land. Several times we tried to set the timer and get a photo with all three of us in it, but, inevitably, I was tumbling in one or the other direction having rushed at them over rocks to get "set" for the picture in the few seconds the camera gave me. So we have a series of photographs with me falling and my family laughing, all testimonies to the joys and beauties of that day.

As we began to "summit" on our return, my son found a fishing line and began pulling it. Little by little it emerged from the water and then back up onto the land, through a small bush and then under a stone, a testimony of its own to a fisherman probably no more experienced than we, also just wanting to go down this slope and touch those waters. Either the fish whipped him, the waters, or his own inexperience, but he left behind enough line for us to re-string our own poles at home with "genuine, authentic, Blackfoot line." I think the perch and crappies in Georgia will jump at a chance to bite on this one.

Beautiful, poetic world. Spring has brought out the playful side of Mother Nature. She pulses forward, throwing our silly accoutrements back at us one by one. I wonder what we left behind on the Blackfoot. Certainly, we left our footprints, but I suspect a little piece of our hearts and peals of laughter got trapped there as well, as we took those pictures. Maybe later this spring when some inexperienced, but fortunate fisherman arrives at this little sacred spot, he will find some of our joy and laughter from yesterday and it will fill his soul as full as the other man's fishing line filled ours with joyful laughter.

"I see skies of blue, and clouds of white… and I think to myself…what a wonderful world."

Spring Grass

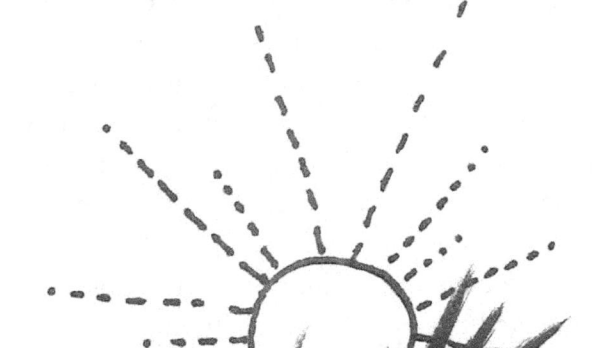

Saturday, March 30: (33°F, low, sunny; 62°F, high)

Time accelerates for me at the end. The morning starts like always and then we go off to see something and just as we seem to get started, the sun begins to descend in the sky and my watch shows unrealistic advances. There is a sort of desperation about leaving a place you love that you think you might never be able to see again. Writ small, it is like a death where the last dying gasps must be savored deeply. And it causes me to think more expansively and take more risks with what remains. Tethered to our work and school schedules, this last release puts me in motion like an explorer with worlds to conquer before she falls over the ends of the map.

For several weeks we had heard about how beautiful the drive is to Philipsburg. We decided to cut through a ranching settlement called Helmville and head to this "scenic place" to the south and see for ourselves. (I find it hard to believe anyone could mark anything specific in Montana as "scenic," since the whole state is marked by unimaginable beauty everywhere. We didn't find this could compete with the primeval beauty of Paradise or the majestic Flathead Lake in Polson or the stark, daunting beauty of Chinook, or the frontier ruggedness of Kalispell, or the…. Well, you get it.) We arrived in Philipsburg, bought candy at the "world's greatest candy store" and then felt unsatisfied and uncontained by this last day of travel in Montana.

Since roads were in good condition overall and I had heard on the radio that all passes were dry today, I diverted the car and we began a true journey, the kind that you do not plan, where everything is *yapa*. We headed southward to Anaconda where we ate pasties that were good enough to make me want to move there permanently, then headed westward on a county road over the Continental Divide and onto a plain so wide that it made us feel dizzy and disoriented. We stopped at Wisdom for a coffee in the Hook and Horn Trading Post and then on to Big Hole, where we heard the story of the Nez Perce Trail and the tragedy of that day not so long ago that still grips the hearts and minds of every visitor. The ranger, amused by our joy, offered us fresh roasted camas roots like those that the Corps of Discovery ate not so far from this place. They were earthy and delicious. We couldn't go out onto the grounds because of deep snow, but from the crow's nest area of the Visitor's Center we were able to imagine this place deeply.

We stayed there a bit too long to be practical, but that is what journeys are all about. My son kept asking questions and gazing onto the plains around us trying to recreate what happened here in his mind and trying so hard to understand it all. History always conjures up emotion – if we truly listen to the past, we cannot be passive. The scenes burst out in our minds and we re-play them with all the advantages of God. We wonder how this could have happened, but mostly, we wonder if we are in history's next scene playing as dismal a role as our ancestors once did. For a brief moment, it distills the cloudiness of our lives.

We left Big Hole as the sun began to decline, stopped a short distance away to walk a few yards on the Nez Perce Trail and imagined the fear and determination they must have felt while traveling this way at that fateful time, and then we headed back toward our Valley, now some four hours away.

Sunday, March 31: (27°F, low, clear - ....)

Well, today is it. Today marks 75 days of being in this lovely state of being - sometimes with burdens, sometimes with delight, but always with gratitude. Deep gratitude.

Montana Winter Days

I walked Kalispell on the logging road in the cold of a clear, imminently sunny day. Clear days have been rare here over the last 10 weeks, but it is Easter and that is fitting. I didn't originally plan for Easter to be our last day here. In fact, I didn't consult the meaning of the days anywhere but on the school calendar. Leaving now puts my son back in school in Georgia by the beginning of their 4th quarter. After we got here we saw what this last day would be. I think this is fortuitous. Our last day should be a "high" church day. After all, it was this little church that drew me back as much as the mountains, the snow, the wide spaces, daunting beauty, and the idea of being "in the real West." During our last church service, Pastor asked everyone to form a hand-held circle and they sang "Blest Be the Tie that Binds" as our farewell. What a fitting dismissal. Indeed, the ties that bind are deep and strong and enduring. I feel them all around me.

The greatest wonder of this journey is that it has caused me to see my life in altered perspective. Away, we can gaze at it all expansively. I have thought so much about my life in Carrollton over these last few days – my little porch, my rocking chair, the raised garden that grows beautiful tomato foliage but bears little fruit, our routines, our friends, the tall stately pines that mark our back forest, our dear neighbors who have accompanied us through both successes and failures, deaths and adoption, my students whose faces I see collaged over the many years I have taught there, some of them very nearly part of my family, the piano teachers, the grocery clerks who we know by name, our beloved park where we walk, swim, and often sup. It is all there. It draws me. It is home. I leave this treasured place feeling drawn back to my roots and my belonging. The mourning is subsiding because I now see something that I know by heart.

As I sit here this last day writing, two healthy cats nap nearby, two dogs snore lightly on the sofa, the shower runs for my mother's bath, and I hear humming out along the side of the house where my son is playing. It is still 27 degrees, but the sun has rimmed the mountains surrounding us, the still-frozen lake in front of the cabin is beginning to shimmer, the grass is turning a lovely green, and the world outside the window seems poised and eager with expectation. Spring is now resident here in the Valley and it is defined by action and energy and bountifulness. We leave renewed and reborn just like the world outside our cabin. And now when I think of home "from the other side," I will also see this little cabin in my mind's eye with its woodsy yard, the logging road behind, our dear neighbors and friends, the shimmering lake, and "these shining mountains" from inside my heart. All *yapa*, all overflowing everywhere.

Southbound

Acknowledgements

    This incredible journey could not have occurred without the wonderful people of Montana. Everywhere we traveled and everyone we met taught us and accompanied us along the way in profound and meaningful ways. I especially thank those who shared their homes with us for rentals during both stays in Montana, Keith & Marilyn and Tony & Jenny. Certainly we could not have lived this dream if you had not been willing to take a risk on us (and our pets) without having ever met us. However, I am most deeply indebted to the anonymous community members of the small towns where we lived during the winters of 2006 and 2013. Our lives have been changed in beautiful ways by your friendships. You made a difference.

    I also thank the illustrator of this little book, my uncle, Wayland Moore, who first encouraged me to go to Montana. His colorful weekly letters and illuminating sketches prompted many of my stories, as I would try to remember things to tell him. Working with him inspires me. Instead of holding on to his talents as commodities, he casts them abroad in the widest manner, sharing himself openly and freely with everyone around him, crafting a world more beautiful than what he first encountered.

    Finally, I thank my little family – Mumsie and Joseph. Because you were "fierce travelers" willing to go where I led, we were able to have the adventure of our lives more than once. Since completing this manuscript, my mother has "slipped the surly bonds of earth" and so I dedicate this work to her love, vision, and spirit which will always live on in Joseph and me. And I dedicate it to Joseph in anticipation of the many travels I trust we will still make together – this time under his leadership. Life remains a beautiful journey even in the face of sadness.

Marjorie M. Snipes

www.ingramcontent.com/pod-product-compliance
Lightning Source LLC
LaVergne TN
LVHW020929090426
835512LV00020B/3272